ITALIAN
REGIONAL
COOKING

ITALIAN REGIONAL COOKING

A STEP-BY-STEP CULINARY TOUR OF THE BEST OF ITALY

CARLA CAPALBO

PHOTOGRAPHY BY AMANDA HEYWOOD

southwater

This edition is published by Southwater

Southwater is an imprint of
Anness Publishing Limited
Hermes House
88–89 Blackfriars Road
London SE1 8HA
tel. 020 7401 2077
fax 020 7633 9499

Distributed in the UK by
The Manning Partnership
251–253 London Road East
Batheaston
Bath BA1 7RL
tel. 01225 852 727
fax 01225 852 852

Distributed in the USA by
Anness Publishing Inc.
27 West 20th Street
Suite 504
New York
NY 10011
tel. 212 807 6739
fax 212 807 6813

Distributed in Australia by
Sandstone Publishing
Unit 1
360 Norton Street
Leichhardt
New South Wales 2040
tel. 02 9560 7888
fax 02 9560 7488

10 9 8 7 6 5 4 3 2 1

Publisher: Joanna Lorenz
Project Editor: Lindsay Porter
Designers: Patrick Mcleavey and Jo Brewer
Photographer: Amanda Heywood
Prop styling: Amanda Heywood, Carla Capalbo
Assistand Home Economists: Marilyn Forbes,
Beverly Le Blanc, Wallace Heim

MEASUREMENTS
Three sets of measurements have been provided in the
recipes here, in the following order: Metric, Imperial
and American. It is essential that units of measurement
are not mixed within each recipe. Where conversions
result in awkward numbers, these have been rounded
for convenience but are still accurate enough for
successful results.

Previously published as *The Best of Italian Regional Cooking* and as
part of a larger compendium, *The Ultimate Italian Cookbook*.

CONTENTS

INTRODUCTION

Italy is a country of great diversity. Its long Mediterranean coastline encloses a landscape of fertile plains, forest-covered mountains and arid rocks. From the hot, dry south to the cool Alpine foothills, the climate varies markedly. So do the local crops: rice, maize and ham are northern staples, while olives, durum wheat and tomatoes thrive in the southern heat.

Italy's many kingdom's, states and duchies were unified as a nation in 1861. Each region had distinct linguistic and cultural differences, still present in the culinary practices today. Despite the advent of industrialization and mass-marketing, traditional foods are still central to the cultural identity of each region. This is partly due to the way in which recipes are learned: orally passed from generation to generation, and rarely written down in cookbooks, they survive in families for years with little or no changes made to them.

A great deal of Italian food comes from this *contadino*, or peasant, heritage. The best combines fresh ingredients with simple cooking techniques. Meats, fish and vegetables are flavored with herbs and olive oil, and often broiled or baked. Aromatic sauces can often be assembled in the time it takes pasta to boil. Many of these recipes can be prepared quickly and economically.

The Italian diet, which is high in vegetables and carbohydrates and low in animal fat, is a healthy one. It also tastes exceptionally good.

Fresh Produce

Italian cooking is based on the creative use of fresh, seasonal ingredients. Vegetables and herbs play central roles in almost every aspect of the menu. In the markets, there is a sense of anticipation at the beginning of each new season, heralded by the arrival, on the beautifully displayed stalls, or the year's first artichokes, olives, chestnuts or wild mushrooms. Seasonal recipes come to the fore and make the most of available produce.

Many of the vegetables once considered exotically Mediterranean are now readily available in the markets and supermarkets of most countries. Fennel and eggplant, peppers, zucchini and radicchio are now increasingly present in pasta sauces, soups and pizzas, as well as wonderful accents to meat and fish.

Wherever you shop, look for the freshest possible fruits and vegetables. Choose unblemished, firm, sun-ripened produce, preferably locally or organically grown. Fresh herbs like basil, parsley and sage are easy to cultivate in window boxes and gardens and have an infinitely finer flavor than their dried counterparts. Italian cuisine is not a complicated or sophisticated style of cooking, but your recipes will benefit immeasurably by starting with the best quality ingredients you can find.

Below: *Italian cuisine does not rely on unusual produce, but it must be as fresh as possible.*

Kitchen Cupboard Ingredients

Perhaps the single most important ingredient in a modern Italian kitchen is olive oil. The fruity flavor of a fine extra-virgin olive oil perfumes any dish it is used in, from pesto sauce to the simplest salad dressing. Buy the best olive oil you can afford: one bottle goes a long way and makes a huge difference to any recipe.

Balsamic vinegar has only recently become widely available outside of Italy. Made by the slow wood-aging process of wine vinegar, the finest varieties are deliciously mellow and fragrant. The taste is quite sweet and concentrated, so only a little is needed.

Porcini mushrooms are found in the woods in various parts of Europe in autumn. They can be eaten cooked fresh, or sliced thinly and dried in the sun or in special ovens. A few dried porcini soaked in water adds a deliciously woodsy flavor.

Olives are one of Italy's most wonderful native ingredients. Unfortunately, freshly cured olives do not travel very well, and many of the most delicious varieties are not available outside the Mediterranean. Sample canned or bottled olives before adding them to sauces as they sometimes acquire an unpleasant metallic taste that could spoil the flavor of the dish.

A typical Italian store cupboard also contains a supply of dried, natural ingredients. Dried beans, lentils and

Above: *An Italian kitchen might have a selection of dried beans, pulses and rice; olives, olive oil and good quality vinegar; as well as dried spices and other flavorings.*

grains are stored in air-tight dispensers for use in soups and stews. Polenta, the coarsely ground yellow maize, is a staple of the northern Italian diet, as is the rice used to make risotto. Of the special varieties grown in the area for this purpose, the best known are Arborio, Vialone Nano and Carnaroli.

Capers, pine nuts, sun-dried tomatoes, dried chilies, juniper berries and fennel seeds are some of the other ingredients commonly used to give Italian dishes their characteristic flavors, and are good basics to keep in the kitchen cupboard.

Meats and Cheeses

Antipasti do not always entail large amounts of preparation, and are often simply composed of the ingredients typical of the region. A popular antipasto consists of a plate of mixed prepared meats and sausages. Salamis, pancetta, air-dried bresaola, coppa and mortadella sausages are some of the meats most commonly used in Italy, often served with an accompaniment of crusty bread and butter. Prosciutto crudo, raw Parma ham, is the most prized of all meats, and is delicious served thinly sliced with ripe melon or fresh figs.

An Italian meal is more likely to end with a selection of cheeses and fruit than a sweet dessert. Among the huge variety of cheeses, the following are some of the best known:

Gorgonzola is made in Lombardy and is a creamy blue cheese. It has a mild flavor when young, which becomes stronger with maturity.

Mascarpone is a rich, triple-cream cheese with a mild flavor. It is often used in desserts as a substitute for whipped cream.

Mozzarella is a fresh, white cheese made from water buffalos, or, more commonly, cows milk. The texture is soft and chewy and the taste mild.

Parmesan is a long-aged, full-flavored cheese with a hard rind, used for both grating and eating in slivers. The large wheels are aged from 18–36 months. Fresh Parmesan is superb, and is incomparably better than the ready-grated varieties sold pre-packaged.

Pecorino is made from ewes milk, and comes in two main types, Pecorino Romano and Pecorino Toscano. This salted, sharp-flavored cheese is widely used for dessert eating, and for grating when mature.

Scamorza is made from cows milk. Its distinctive shape is due to being hung from a string during aging.

Below: *A typical Italian meal might include cured meat as an antipasto, and finish with cheese instead of a sweet dessert.*

Equipment

1 *Earthenware pot*. Excellent for slow-cooking stews, soups or sauces. Can be used either in the oven or on top of the stove with a metal heat diffuser under it to discourage cracking. Many shapes and sizes are available. To season an earthenware pot before using it for the first time, immerse in cold water overnight. Remove from the water and rub the unglazed bottom with garlic. Fill with water and bring slowly to a boil. Discard the water. Repeat, changing the water, until the 'earth' taste disappears.

2 *Pasta rolling pin*. A length of doweling 2 in in diameter can also be used. Smooth with sandpaper before using for the first time.

3 *Pestle and mortar*. For hand-grinding spices, pepper, herbs and breadcrumbs.

4 *Hand food mill*. Excellent for soups, sauces and tomato 'passata': the pulp passes through the holes leaving the seeds and skin behind.

5 *Colander*. Indispensable for draining hot pasta and vegetables.

6 *Parmesan cheese knife*. In Italy Parmesan is not cut with a conventional knife, but broken off the large cheese wheels using this kind of wedge. Insert the point and apply pressure.

7 *Pizza cutting wheel*. Useful for cutting slices, although a sharp knife may also be used.

8 *Spatula*. Very useful for spreading and smoothing.

9 *Spaghetti spoon*. The wooden 'teeth' catch the spaghetti strands as they boil.

10 *Meat hammer*. For pounding escalops. Also useful for crushing nuts and spices.

11 *Pasta machine*. Many are available, including electric and industrial models. Most have an adjustable roller width and thin and wide noodle cutters.

12 *Icing nozzles*. For piping decorations, garnishes, etc. Use with a nylon or paper pastry bag.

13 *Wide vegetable peeler*. Very easy to use for all sizes of vegetable.

14 *Italian gelato scoop*. Good for soft ices that are not too solid.

15 *Ice cream scoop*. Better for firm and well-frozen ice creams.

16 *Olive pitter*. Can also be used for pitting cherries.

17 *Whisk*. Excellent for smoothing sauces, beating egg whites.

18 *Fluted pastry cutter*. For cutting fresh pasta or pastry.

19 *Cookie cutter*. Also used for cutting fresh pasta shapes.

How to Make Egg Pasta by Hand

This classic recipe for egg noodles from Emilia-Romagna calls for just three ingredients: flour and eggs, with a little salt. In other regions of Italy water, milk or oil are sometimes added. Use plain unbleached white flour, and large eggs. As a general guide, use ½ cup of flour to each egg Quantities will vary with the exact size of the eggs.

To serve 3–4
2 eggs, salt
1 cup flour

To serve 4–6
3 eggs, salt
1½ cups flour

To serve 6–8
4 eggs, salt
2 cups flour

1 ▲ Place the flour in the center of a clean smooth work surface. Make a well in the middle. Break the eggs into the well. Add a pinch of salt.

2 Start beating the eggs with a fork, gradually drawing the flour from the inside walls of the well. As the paste thickens, continue the mixing with your hands. Incorporate as much flour as possible until the mixture forms a mass. It will still be lumpy. If it still sticks to your hands, add a little more flour. Set the dough aside. Scrape off all traces of the dough from the work surface until it is perfectly smooth. Wash and dry your hands.

About Pasta

Most pasta is made from durum wheat flour and water – durum is a special kind of wheat with a very high protein content. Egg pasta, *pasta all'uova*, contains flour and eggs, and is used for flat noodles such as tagliatelle, or for lasagne. Very little whole wheat pasta is eaten in Italy, but it is quite popular in other countries.

All these types of pasta are available dried in packets, and will keep almost indefinitely. Fresh pasta is now more widely available and can be bought in most supermarkets. It can be very good, but can never compare to home-made egg pasta.

Pasta comes in countless shapes and sizes. It is very difficult to give a definite list, as the names for the shapes vary from country to country. In some cases, just within Italy, the same shape can appear with several different names, depending upon which region it is in. The pasta shapes called for in this book, as well as many others, are illustrated in the introduction. The most common names have been listed.

Most of the recipes in this book specify the pasta shape most appropriate for a particular sauce. They can, of course, be replaced with another kind. A general rule is that long pasta goes better with tomato or thinner sauces, while short pasta is best for chunkier, meatier sauces. But this rule should not be followed too rigidly. Part of the fun of cooking and eating pasta is in the endless combinations of sauce and pasta shapes.

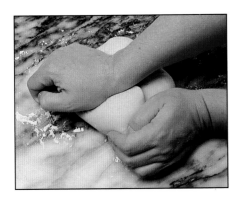

3 ▲ Lightly flour the work surface. Knead the dough by pressing it away from you with the heel of your hands, and then folding it over towards you. Repeat this action over and over, turning the dough as you knead. Work for about 10 minutes, or until the dough is smooth and elastic.

4 ▲ If you are using more than 2 eggs, divide the dough in half. Flour the rolling pin and the work surface. Pat the dough into a disc and begin rolling it out into a flat circle, rotating it one quarter turn after each roll to keep its shape round. Roll until the disc is about ⅛ in thick.

5 ▲ Roll out the dough until it is paper-thin by rolling up onto the

rolling pin and simultaneously giving a sideways stretching with the hands. Wrap the near edge of the dough around the center of the rolling pin, and begin rolling the dough up away from you. As you roll back and forth, slide your hands from the center towards the outer edges of the pin, stretching and thinning out the pasta.

6 ▲ Quickly repeat these movements until about two-thirds of the sheet of pasta is wrapped around the pin. Lift and turn the wrapped pasta sheet about 45° before unrolling it. Repeat the rolling and stretching process, starting from a new point of the sheet each time to keep it evenly thin. By the end (this process should not last more than 8 to 10 minutes or the dough will lose its elasticity) the whole sheet should be smooth and almost transparent. If the dough is still sticky, lightly flour your hands as you continue rolling and stretching.

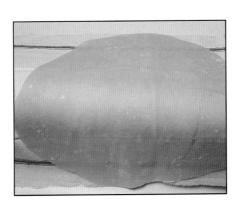

7 ▲ If you are making noodles (tagliatelle, fettuccine etc.) lay a clean dish towel on a table or other flat surface, and unroll the pasta sheet on it, letting about a third of the sheet hang over the edge of the table. Rotate

the dough every 10 minutes. Roll out the second sheet of dough if you are using more than 2 eggs. After 25–30 minutes the pasta will have dried enough to cut. Do not overdry or the pasta will crack as it is cut.

8 ▲ To cut tagliatelle, fettuccine or tagliolini, fold the sheet of pasta into a flat roll about 4 in wide. Cut across the roll to form noodles of the desired width. Tagliolini is ⅛ in; Fettuccine is ⅙ in; Tagliatelle is ¼ in. After cutting, open out the noodles, and let them dry for about 5 minutes before cooking. These noodles may be stored for some weeks without refrigeration. Allow them to dry completely before storing them, uncovered, in a dry cupboard.

9 ▲ To cut the pasta for lasagne or pappardelle, do not fold or dry the rolled out dough. Lasagne is made by cutting rectangles approximately 5 in by 3½ in. Pappardelle are large noodles cut with a fluted pastry wheel. They are about ¾ in wide.

Egg Pasta Made by Machine

Making pasta with a machine is quick and easy. The results are perhaps not quite as fine as with handmade pasta, but they are certainly better than store-bought pastas.

You will need a pasta-making machine, either hand-cranked or electric. Use the same proportions of eggs, flours and salt as for Handmade Egg Pasta.

1 ▲ Place the flour in the center of a clean smooth work surface. Make a well in the middle. Break the eggs into the well. Add a pinch of salt. Start beating the eggs with a fork, gradually drawing the flour from the inside walls of the well. As the paste thickens, continue mixing with your hands. Incorporate as much flour as possible until the mixture forms a mass. It will still be lumpy. If it sticks to your hands, add a little more flour. Set the dough aside and scrape the work surface clean.

2 ▲ Set the machine rollers at their widest (kneading) setting. Pull off a piece of dough the size of a small

orange. Place the remaining dough between two soup plates. Feed the dough through the rollers. Fold it in half, end to end, and feed it through again 7 or 8 times, turning it and folding it over after each kneading. The dough should be smooth and fairly evenly rectangular. If it sticks to the machine, brush with flour. Lay it out on a lightly floured work surface or on a clean dish towel, and repeat with the remaining dough, broken into pieces the same size.

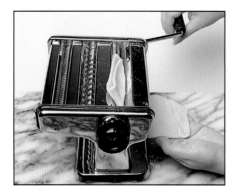

3 ▲ Adjust the machine to the next line setting. Feed each strip through once only, and replace on the drying surface. Keep them in the order in which they were first kneaded.

4 ▲ Reset the machine to the next setting. Repeat, passing each strip through once. Repeat for each remaining roller setting until the pasta is the right thickness – for most purposes this is given by the next to last setting, except for very delicate strips such as tagliolini, or for ravioli. If the pasta strips get too long, cut them in half to facilitate handling.

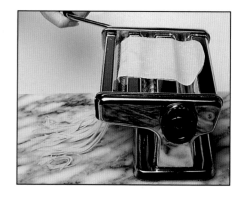

5 ▲ When all the strips are the desired thickness they may be machine-cut into noodles, or hand-cut for lasagne or pappardelle, as described for handmade pasta earlier. When making noodles, be sure the pasta is fairly dry, but not brittle, or the noodles may stick togther when cut. Select the desired width of cutter, and feed the strips through.

6 Separate the noodles, and leave to dry for at least 15 minutes before using. They may be stored for some weeks without refrigeration. Allow them to dry completely before storing them, uncovered, in a dry cupboard. They may also be frozen, first loose on trays and then packed together.

7 If you are making stuffed pasta (ravioli, cannelloni etc.) do not let the pasta strips dry out before filling them, but proceed immediately with the individual recipes.

~ PASTA VERDE ~

Follow the same recipe, adding ¼ cup cooked, very finely chopped spinach after having been squeezed very dry) to the eggs and flour. You may have to add a little more flour to absorb the moisture from the spinach. This pasta is very suitable for stuffed recipes, as it seals better than plain egg pasta.

How to Cook Dried Pasta

Store-bought and home-made pasta are cooked in the same way, though the timings vary greatly. Home-made pasta cooks virtually in the time it takes for the water to return to a boil after it is put in.

1 Always cook pasta in a large pot with a generous amount of rapidly boiling water. Use at least 5 cups of water to each ½ cup pasta.

2 ▲ The water should be salted at least 2 minutes before the pasta is added, to give the salt time to dissolve. Add about 1½ tbsp salt per 2 cups of pasta. You may want to vary the saltiness of the cooking water.

3 ▲ Drop the pasta into the boiling water all at once. Use a wooden spoon to help ease long pasta in as it softens, to prevent it from breaking. Stir frequently to prevent the pasta sticking to itself or to the pan. Cook the pasta at a fast boil, but be prepared to lower the heat if it boils over.

4 Timing is critical in pasta cooking. Follow package indications for store-bought pasta, but it is best in all cases to test for doneness by tasting, several times if necessary. In Italy pasta is always eaten *al dente*, which mens firm to the bite. Cooked this way it is just tender, but its "soul" (the innermost part) is still firm.

5 ▲ Place a colander in the sink before the pasta has finished cooking. As soon as the pasta tastes done, tip it all into the colander (you may first want to reserve a cupful of the hot cooking water to add to the sauce if it needs thinning). Shake the colander lightly to remove most but not all of the cooking water. Pasta should never be over-drained.

6 ▲ Quickly turn the pasta into a warmed serving dish, and immediately toss it with a little butter or oil, or the prepared sauce. Alternatively, turn it into the cooking pan with the sauce, where it will be cooked for 1–2 minutes more as it is mixed into the sauce. Never allow pasta to sit undressed, as it will stick together and become unpalatable.

How to Cook Egg Pasta

Fresh egg pasta, especially home-made, cooks very much faster than dried pasta. Make sure everything is ready (the sauce, serving dishes, etc.) before you start boiling egg pasta, as there will not be time once the cooking starts, and egg pasta becomes soft and mushy very quickly.

1 Always cook pasta in a large pot with a generous amount of rapidly boiling water. Use at least 5 cups of water to a quantity of pasta made with 1 cup of flour. Salt the water as for dried pasta.

2 ▲ Drop the pasta into the boiling water all at once. Stir gently to prevent the pasta sticking to itself or to the pan. Cook the pasta at a fast boil.

3 ▲ Freshly made pasta can be done as little as 15 seconds after their cooking water comes back to a boil. Stuffed pasta takes a few minutes longer. When done, tip the pasta into the colander and proceed as for dried pasta.

Pasta

Pasta in its many forms is a staple of Italian cuisine. These are just some of the varieties available.

1 *Alfabeto.* Small alphabet pasta for soups.

2 *Anellini.* Little rings used in soups and broth.

3 *Canneroni.* Pasta rings for thick vegetable soups.

4 *Capellini.* Very fine "angel hair" pasta, can be broken up and used in broths.

5 *Chifferi piccoli lisci.* Smooth, macaroni-like pasta used in baked dishes.

6 *Chifferi piccoli rigati.* Ridged version of the above.

7 *Conchigliette.* Small shells used in soups.

8 *Conchigliette rigati.* Small, ridged shells used in thick soups.

9 *Conchiglioni rigati.* Large, ridged shells used for stuffing and baking.

10 *Ditali.* Used in soups, traditionally with dried beans.

11 *Ditalini.* Soup pasta, smaller than ditali.

12 *Ditalini lisci.* Smooth ditalini, also used in soups.

13 *Elicoidali.* Good for baked dishes, or those with chunky sauces.

14 *Fagiolini.* "String beans" used in soups.

15 *Farfalle.* Butterflies or bows. Excellent with shrimp and peas and in cold pasta salads.

16 *Fusilli.* These spirals are ideal with tomato and vegetable sauces.

17 *Fusilli integrali.* Whole wheat spirals. Good hot or cold with thick vegetable sauces.

18 *Fusillata casareccia.* The twisted shape is good with tomato sauce.

19 *Gnocchi.* Shells for chunky vegetable or meat sauces. Gnocchi tricolori (19a) is flavored with tomato and spinach.

20 *Gnocchi integrali.* Whole wheat shells popular in vegetarian dishes, hot or cold.

21 *Gnocchetti sardi.* Sardinian shells. Good with lamb or fish sauces.

22 *Lasagne doppia riccia.* Frilly-edged lasagne. This is a dry version of the popular egg pasta, used for stuffed and baked dishes.

23 *Lasagne verdi.* Spinach gives this lasagne its green color.

24 *Lingue di passero, Bavette.* Traditionally paired with the classic pesto sauce.

25 *Linguine, Bavettine.* This finer version of lingue de passoro is good with fish sauces.

26 *Lumache rigate grandi.* These large, ridged "snails" are suitable for thick sauces with strong flavors such as olives and capers. Also good for pasta salads.

27 *Macaroni.* This is the English version of Italian maccherone, most popular baked with cheese.

28 *Mafaldine.* This is often eaten with sauces made from soft cheeses, such as ricotta.

29 *Mezze penne rigate tricolori.* The pasta is tinted with tomato and spinach to produce Italy's favorite colors.

30 *Orecchiette.* Dry version of the traditionally hand-made pasta popular in the south of Italy. Cooked with green vegetables.

31 *Penne lisce.* Quills or pens. Cut diagonally to catch more sauce.

32 *Penne rigate.* Ridged quills, a favorite shape in Italy. Great with tomato sauces.

33 *Pennoni rigati.* Large ridged quills. Good for baked dishes.

34 *Peperini.* Little pasta dots to add to broth or soups.

35 *Perciatellini.* This is a hollow spaghetti. Can be used with any of the usual spaghetti sauces.

36 *Pipe rigate.* "Ridged pipes". Good for thick, chunky sauces with peas or lentils.

37 *Puntalette.* For adding to soups and broths.

38 *Rigatoni.* Often baked with meat sauces and cheeses. Mezza rigatoni (38a) are smaller in size.

39 *Ruote.* Pasta wheels, always popular with children.

40 *Spaghetti integrali.* Whole wheat version of spaghetti (40a), more popular abroad than in Italy.

41 *Spaghettini.* Finer version of spaghetti, good with delicate sauces.

42 *Stelline.* Little stars, another small soup pasta.

43 *Tagliatelle.* Dried egg noodles, good with creamy sauces.

44 *Tagliatelle verdi.* Dried spinach-flavored egg noodles.

45 *Tomato spirals.* Specially made tomato-flavored pasta.

46 *Tortellini.* Small dumplings, often cooked and eaten in broth.

47 *Tortelloni.* Pasta dumplings stuffed with meats or cheeses.

48 *Zite.* A long hollow pasta often used with fish or tomato sauces.

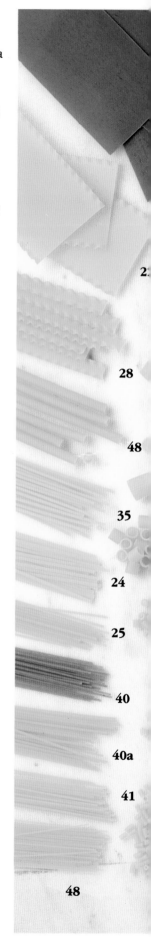

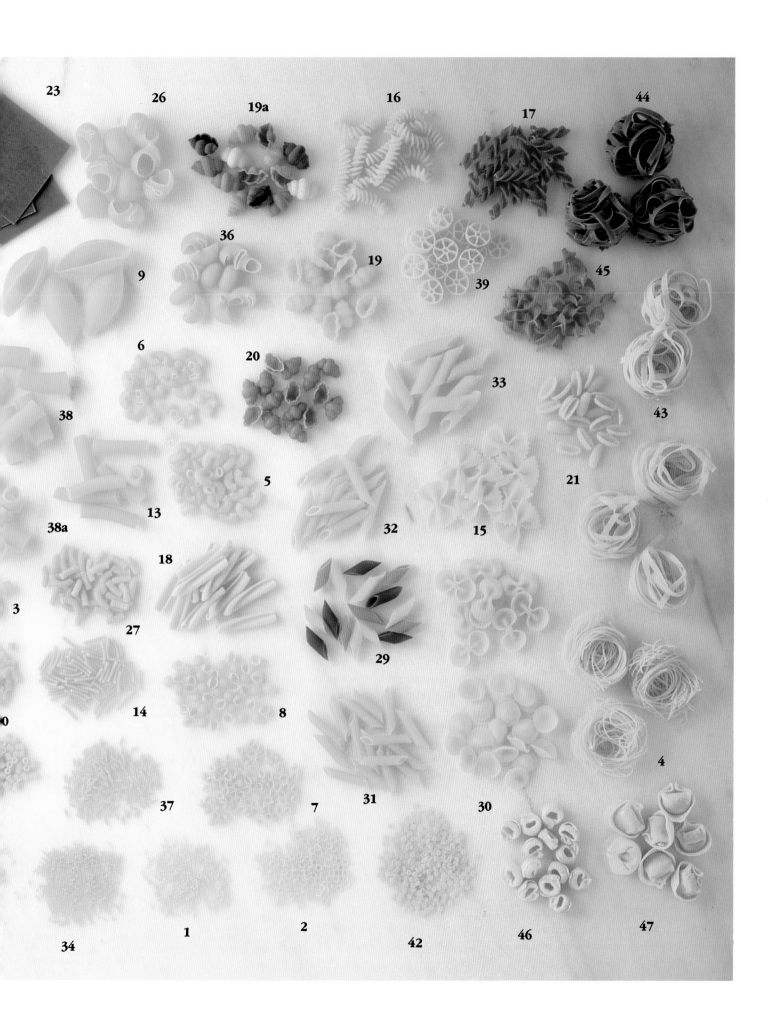

Basic Pizza Dough

Pizza dough is leavened with yeast. It usually rises once before being rolled out and filled. The dough can be baked in pizza pans or baked directly on a flat cookie sheet.

Ingredients

2½ tbsp fresh cake yeast or 1 package
    dry yeast
1 cup lukewarm water
pinch of sugar
1 tsp salt
3–3½ cups unbleached white flour
serves 4 as a main course or 8 as an appetizer

1 ▲ Warm a medium mixing bowl by swirling some hot water in it. Drain. Place the yeast in the bowl, and pour on the warm water. Stir in the sugar, mix with a fork, and allow to stand until the yeast has dissolved and starts to foam, 5–10 minutes.

2 ▲ Use a wooden spoon to mix in the salt and about one-third of the flour. Mix in another third of the flour, stirring with the spoon until the dough forms a mass and begins to pull away from the sides of the bowl.

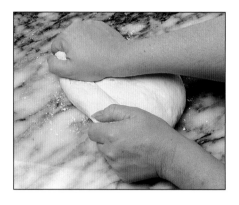

3 ▲ Sprinkle some of the remaining flour onto a smooth work surface. Remove the dough from the bowl and begin to knead it, working in the remaining flour a little at a time. Knead for 8–10 minutes. By the end the dough should be elastic and smooth. Form it into a ball.

4 Lightly oil a mixing bowl. Place the dough in the bowl. Stretch a moistened and wrung-out dish towel across the top of the bowl, and leave it to stand in a warm place until the dough has doubled in volume, about 40–50 minutes or more, depending on the type of yeast used. (If you do not have a warm enough place, turn the oven on to medium heat for 10 minutes before you knead the dough. Turn it off. Place the bowl with the dough in it in the turned-off oven with the door closed and let it rise there.) To test whether the dough has risen enough, poke two fingers into the dough. If the indentations remain, the dough is ready.

5 ▲ Punch the dough down with your fist to release the air. Knead for 1–2 minutes.

6 If you want to make 2 medium pizzas, divide the dough into 2 balls. If you want to make 4 individual pizzas (in pans 10½ in in diameter), divide the dough into 4 balls. Pat the ball of dough out into a flat circle on a lightly floured surface. With a rolling pin, roll it out to a thickness of about ⅜–¼ inch. If you are using a pizza pan, roll the dough out about ¼ inch larger than the size of the pan for the rim of the crust.

7 ▲ Place in the lightly oiled pan, folding the extra dough under to make a thicker rim around the edge. If you are baking the pizza without a round pan, press some of the dough from the center of the circle towards the edge, to make a thicker rim. Place it on a lightly oiled flat cookie sheet. The dough is now ready for filling.

~ COOK'S TIP ~

This basic dough can be used for other recipes in this book, such as Focaccia, Breadsticks, Calzone and Sicilian Closed Pizza. The dough may be frozen at the end of step 7, and thawed before filling.

Wholewheat Pizza Dough

Pizza dough can also be made with wholewheat flour, although it is easier to handle and more elastic if a proportion of white flour is used. This dough can be used in any recipe calling for Basic Pizza Dough.

Ingredients
2½ tbsp fresh cake yeast or 1½ tbsp
    active dried yeast
1 cup lukewarm water
pinch of sugar
2 tbsp olive oil
1 tsp salt
1¼ cups plain white flour
2 cups stoneground wholewheat flour
serves 4 as a main course or 8 as an appetizer

1 Warm a medium mixing bowl by swirling some hot water in it. Drain. Place the yeast in the bowl, and pour on the warm water. Stir in the sugar, mix with a fork, and allow to stand until the yeast has dissolved and starts to foam, 5–10 minutes.

2 ▲ Use a wooden spoon to mix in the olive oil and the salt, and the white flour. Mix in about half of the wholewheat flour, stirring with the spoon until the dough forms a mass and begins to pull away from the sides of the bowl.

3 ▲ Proceed with steps 3–7 as for Basic Pizza Dough, punching down the risen dough, and kneading until ready to roll out and place in a pan.

To Make the Dough in a Food Processor

1 ▲ Have all the ingredients ready and measured out. In a small jug or bowl add the yeast to the warm water. Stir in the sugar, and allow to stand until the yeast has dissolved, 5–10 minutes.

2 ▲ Fit the food processor with the metal blades. Place the salt and three-quarters of the flour in the bowl of the food processor. Turn it on, and pour in the yeast mixture and olive oil through the opening at the top. Continue processing until the dough forms one or two balls. Turn the machine off, open it, and touch the dough. If it still feels sticky, add a little more flour, and process again until it is incorporated.

3 ▲ Remove the dough from the processor. Knead it for about 2–3 minutes on a surface dusted with the remaining flour. Form it into a ball. Proceed with Step 4 of Basic Pizza Dough.

NORTHERN ITALY

Northern Italy consists of eight romantically named regions: Valla d'Aosta; Piedmont; Liguria; Lombardi; Trentino-Alto Adige; Friuli-Venizia Giulia; Venetia and Emilia-Romagna.

In this fertile land where Italy meets the rest of Europe, more continental influences and exchanges are in evidence, in staple ingredients such as rice (especially in the local *risottos*), cornmeal (in *polenta*) and a much higher incidence of cheeses and dairy products (such as Piedmontese *gorgonzola*), red meats, and poultry.

Raw Vegetables with Olive Oil Dip   *Pinzimonio*

Use a combination of any fresh seasonal vegetables for this colorful antipasto from Rome, where the dip usually consists only of olive oil and salt. The vegetables should be raw or lightly blanched, and the olive oil of the best quality available.

Ingredients
3 large carrots, peeled
2 fennel bulbs
6 tender stalks celery
1 pepper
12 radishes, trimmed of roots
2 large tomatoes, or 12 cherry tomatoes
8 scallions
12 small cauliflower florets
For the dip
½ cup extra-virgin olive oil
salt and freshly ground black pepper
3 tbsp fresh lemon juice (optional)
4 leaves fresh basil, torn into small pieces
   (optional)
serves 6–8

1 Prepare the vegetables by slicing the carrots, fennel, celery and pepper into small sticks.

2 ▲ Cut the large tomatoes into sections if using. Trim the roots and dark green leaves from the scallions. Arrange the vegetables on a large platter, leaving a space in the center for the dip.

3 ▲ Make the dip by pouring the olive oil into a small bowl. Add salt and pepper. Stir in the lemon juice and basil, if using. Place the bowl in the center of the vegetable platter.

Celery Stuffed with Gorgonzola   *Sedano ripieno di Gorgonzola*

These celery stalks are very easy to make. Serve them with drinks, or take them to a picnic.

Ingredients
12 crisp stalks celery, leaves left on
½ cup Gorgonzola cheese
½ cup cream cheese
fresh chives, to garnish
serves 4–6

1 ▲ Wash and dry the celery stalks, and trim the root ends.

2 ▲ In a small bowl, mash the cheeses together until smooth.

3 Fill the celery stalks with the cheese mixture, using a spatula to smooth the filling. Chill before serving. Garnish with chopped chives.

Crostini with Cheese

Crostini con formaggio

Crostini are small pieces of toasted bread. They can be made with various toppings, and are served hot or cold with drinks. This cheese-topped version is always popular.

Ingredients

4–6 slices day-old white or brown bread
¾ cup thinly sliced cheese (fontina,
    Cheddar or gruyère)
anchovy fillets
strips of grilled red pepper
freshly ground black pepper
serves 6

1 ▲ Cut the bread into small shapes (triangle, circle, oval, etc.). Preheat the oven to 375°F.

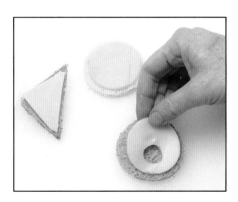

2 ▲ Place a thin slice of cheese on each piece of bread, cutting it to fit.

~ VARIATION ~

For a colorful addition use strips of green or yellow pepper.

3 ▲ Cut the anchovy fillets and strips of pepper into small decorative shapes and place on top of the cheese. Grind a little pepper on each.

4 ▲ Butter a cookie sheet. Place the crostini on it, and bake for 10 minutes, or until the cheese has melted. Serve straight from the oven, or allow to cool before serving.

Crostini with Mussels or Clams   *Crostini con cozze o vongole*

Each of these seafood crostini is topped with a mussel or clam, and then baked. This recipe comes from Genoa. Use fresh seafood whenever possible.

Ingredients

16 large mussels or clams, in their shells
4 large slices bread, 1 in thick
3 tbsp butter
2 tbsp chopped fresh parsley
1 shallot, very finely chopped
olive oil, for brushing
lemon sections, to serve
makes 16

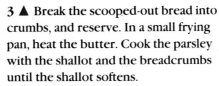

3 ▲ Break the scooped-out bread into crumbs, and reserve. In a small frying pan, heat the butter. Cook the parsley with the shallot and the breadcrumbs until the shallot softens.

4 ▲ Brush each piece of bread with olive oil. Place one mussel or clam in each hollow. Spoon a small amount of the parsley and shallot mixture onto each mollusc. Place on an oiled cookie sheet. Bake for 10 minutes. Serve at once, while still hot, with the lemon sections.

1 ▲ Wash the mussels or clams well in several changes of water. Cut the "beards" off the mussels. Place the shellfish in a saucepan with a cupful of water, and heat until the shells open. (Discard any that do not open.) As soon as they open, lift the molluscs out of the pan. Spoon out of their shells, and set aside. Preheat the oven to 375°F.

2 ▲ Cut the crusts off the bread. Cut each slice into quarters. Scoop out a hollow from the top of each piece large enough to hold a mussel or clam. Do not cut through to the bottom.

Stewed Peppers

Peperonata

This dish originated in the south of Italy, but has become a popular favorite everywhere. It can be eaten as a side dish or appetizer, and makes a delicious filling for a frittata.

Ingredients
4–5 very ripe peppers, preferably red or
    yellow, about 1½ lb
4 tbsp olive oil
2 medium onions, thinly sliced
3 cloves garlic, finely chopped
12 oz plum tomatoes, peeled, seeded and
    chopped
salt and freshly ground black pepper
a few fresh basil leaves
serves 6

1 Wash the peppers. Cut them into quarters, removing the stems and seeds. Slice them into thin strips.

2 ▲ In a large heavy saucepan, heat the oil and sauté the onions until soft (covering the pan will prevent the onions from browning). Add the peppers, and cook for 5–8 minutes over moderate heat, stirring frequently.

3 ▲ Stir in the garlic and tomatoes. Cover the pan, and cook for about 25 minutes, stirring occasionally. The peppers should be soft, but should still hold their shape. Season, tear the basil leaves into pieces, and stir into the peppers. Serve hot or cold.

Broiled Radicchio and Zucchini

Verdure ai ferri

In Italy radicchio is often eaten broiled or barbecued. It is delicious and very easy to prepare.

Ingredients
2–3 firm heads of radicchio, round or long
    type
4 medium zucchini
6 tbsp olive oil
salt and freshly ground black pepper
serves 4

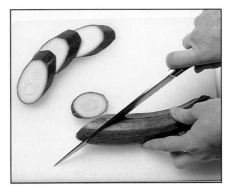

2 ▲ Cut the zucchini into ½ inch diagonal slices.

3 ▲ When the broiler or barbecue is hot, brush the vegetables all over with the oil, and sprinkle with salt and pepper. Cook for 4–5 minutes on each side. Serve alone or as an accompaniment to broiled fish or meats.

1 ▲ Preheat the broiler, or prepare a barbecue. Cut the radicchio in half through the root section or base. If necessary, wash in cold water. Drain.

Zucchine with Sun-dried Tomatoes   *Zucchine con pomodori*

One way to preserve tomatoes for winter is to dry them in the sun, as they do all over southern Italy. These tomatoes have a concentrated, sweet flavor that goes well with zucchine.

Ingredients

10 sun-dried tomatoes, dry or preserved
    in oil and drained
¾ cup warm water
5 tbsp olive oil
1 large onion, finely sliced
2 cloves garlic, finely chopped
2 lb zucchine, cut into thin strips
salt and freshly ground black pepper
serves 6

3 ▲ Stir in the garlic and the zucchine. Cook for about 5 minutes, continuing to stir the mixture.

4 ▲ Stir in the tomatoes and their soaking liquid. Season with salt and pepper. Raise the heat slightly and cook until the zucchine are just tender. Serve hot or cold.

1 ▲ Slice the tomatoes into thin strips. Place in a bowl with the warm water. Allow to stand for 20 minutes.

2 ▲ In a large frying pan or saucepan, heat the oil and stir in the onion. Cook over low to moderate heat until it softens but does not brown.

Stuffed Onions

Cipolle ripiene

These savory onions make a satisfying dish for a light lunch or supper. Small onions could be stuffed and served as an accompaniment to a meat dish.

Ingredients
6 large onions
scant ½ cup ham, cut into small dice
1 egg
½ cup dry breadcrumbs
3 tbsp finely chopped fresh parsley
1 clove garlic, finely chopped
pinch of grated nutmeg
¾ cup grated cheese, such as Parmesan
　or Romano
6 tbsp olive oil
salt and freshly ground black pepper
serves 6

1 Peel the onions without cutting through the base. Cook them in a large pan of boiling water for about 20 minutes. Drain, and refresh in plenty of cold water.

2 ▲ Using a small sharp knife, cut around and scoop out the central section. Remove about half the inside (save it for soup). Lightly salt the empty cavities, and leave the onions to drain upside down.

3 ▲ Preheat the oven to 400°F. In a small bowl, beat the ham into the egg. Stir in the breadcrumbs, parsley, garlic, nutmeg and all but 3 tbsp of the grated cheese. Add 3 tbsp of the oil, and season with salt and pepper.

4 Pat the insides of the onions dry with paper towels. Stuff them using a small spoon. Arrange the onions in one layer in an oiled baking dish.

5 ▲ Sprinkle the tops with the remaining cheese, and sprinkle with oil. Bake for 45 minutes, or until the onions are tender and golden on top.

~ **VARIATION** ~

For a vegetarian version, replace the ham with chopped olives.

Barley and Vegetable Soup

Minestrone d'orzo

This soup comes from the Alto Adige region, in Italy's mountainous north. It is a thick, nourishing and warming winter soup. Serve with crusty bread.

Ingredients
1 cup pearl barley, preferably organic
9 cups fresh or canned beef stock or
    water, or a combination of both
3 tbsp olive oil
2 carrots, finely chopped
1 large onion, finely chopped
2 stalks celery, finely chopped
1 leek, thinly sliced
1 large potato, finely chopped
½ cup diced ham
1 bay leaf
3 tbsp chopped fresh parsley
1 small sprig fresh rosemary
salt and freshly ground black pepper
freshly grated Parmesan cheese, to serve
    (optional)
serves 6–8

1 Pick over the barley, and discard any stones or other particles. Wash it in cold water. Put the barley to soak in cold water for at least 3 hours.

2 Drain the barley and place in a large saucepan with the stock or water. Bring to a boil, lower the heat and simmer for 1 hour. Skim off any scum.

3 ▲ Stir in the oil, all the vegetables and the ham. Add the herbs. If necessary add more water. The ingredients should be covered by at least 1 in. Simmer for 1–1½ hours, or until the vegetables and barley are very tender.

4 ▲ Taste for seasoning, adding salt and pepper as necessary. Serve hot with grated Parmesan, if desired.

~ VARIATION ~

An excellent vegetarian version of this soup can be made by using vegetable stock instead of beef stock, and omitting the ham.

Rice and Broad Bean Soup

Minestra di riso e fave

This thick soup makes the most of fresh broad beans while they are in season. It works well with frozen beans for the rest of the year.

Ingredients
2 lb broad beans in their pods, or 14 oz
    shelled frozen broad beans, thawed
6 tbsp olive oil
1 medium onion, finely chopped
salt and freshly ground black pepper
2 medium tomatoes, peeled and finely
    chopped
1 cup risotto or other non-parboiled rice
2 tbsp butter
4 cups boiling water
freshly grated Parmesan cheese, to serve
    (optional)
serves 4

1 ▲ Shell the beans if they are fresh. Bring a large pan of water to a boil, and blanch the beans, fresh or frozen, for 3–4 minutes. Rinse under cold water, and peel off the skins.

2 Heat the oil in a large saucepan. Add the onion, and cook over low to moderate heat until it softens. Stir in the beans, and cook for about 5 minutes, stirring often to coat them with the oil. Season with salt and pepper. Add the tomatoes, and cook for 5 minutes more, stirring often.

3 Stir in the rice. After 1–2 minutes add the butter, and stir until it melts. Pour in the water, a little at a time, until the whole amount has been added. Taste for seasoning. Continue cooking the soup until the rice is tender. Serve hot, with grated Parmesan if desired.

Linguine with Pesto Sauce

Linguine con pesto

Pesto originates in Liguria, where the sea breezes are said to give the local basil a particularly fine flavor. It is traditionally made with a mortar and pestle, but it is easier to make in a food processor or blender. Freeze any spare pesto in an ice cube tray.

Ingredients

¾ cup fresh basil leaves
3–4 cloves garlic, peeled
3 tbsp pine nuts
½ tsp salt
5 tbsp olive oil
½ cup freshly grated Parmesan cheese
4 tbsp freshly grated pecorino cheese
freshly ground black pepper
1¼ lb linguine
serves 5–6

1 ▲ Place the basil, garlic, pine nuts, salt and olive oil in a blender or food processor and process until smooth. Remove to a bowl. (If desired, the sauce may be frozen at this point, before the cheeses are added).

2 ▲ Stir in the cheeses (use all Parmesan if pecorino is not available). Taste for seasoning.

3 ▲ Cook the pasta in a large pan of rapidly boiling salted water until it is *al dente*. Just before draining it, take about 4 tbsp of the cooking water and stir it into the sauce.

4 Drain the pasta and toss with the sauce. Serve immediately.

Bolognese Meat Sauce

Ragù alla bolognese

This great meat sauce is a speciality of Bologna. It is delicious with tagliatelle or short pastas such as penne or conchiglie as well as spaghetti, and is indispensable in baked lasagne. It keeps well in the refrigerator for several days and can also be frozen.

Ingredients

2 tbsp butter
4 tbsp olive oil
1 medium onion, finely chopped
2 tbsp pancetta or unsmoked bacon, finely chopped
1 carrot, finely sliced
1 stalk celery, finely sliced
1 clove garlic, finely chopped
12 oz lean ground beef
salt and freshly ground black pepper
⅔ cup red wine
½ cup milk
1 × 14 oz can plum tomatoes, chopped, with their juice
1 bay leaf
¼ tsp fresh thyme leaves
for 6 servings of pasta

3 ▲ Pour in the wine, raise the heat slightly, and cook until the liquid evaporates, 3–4 minutes. Add the milk, and cook until it evaporates.

4 ▲ Stir in the tomatoes with their juice, and the herbs. Bring the sauce to a boil. Reduce the heat to low, and simmer, uncovered for 1½–2 hours, stirring occasionally. Correct the seasoning before serving.

1 ▲ Heat the butter and oil in a heavy saucepan or earthenware pot. Add the onion, and cook over moderate heat for 3–4 minutes. Add the pancetta, and cook until the onion is translucent. Stir in the carrot, celery and garlic. Cook 3–4 minutes more.

2 Add the beef, and crumble it into the vegetables with a fork. Stir until the meat loses its red color. Season with salt and pepper.

Baked Lasagne with Meat Sauce

Lasagne al forno

This lasagne made from egg pasta with home-made meat and béchamel sauces is exquisite.

Ingredients
1 recipe Bolognese Meat Sauce
egg pasta sheets made with 3 eggs, or
    1 lb dried lasagne
1 cup grated Parmesan cheese
3 tbsp butter
For the béchamel sauce
3 cups milk
1 bay leaf
3 blades mace
½ cup butter
¾ cup flour
salt and freshly ground black pepper
serves 8–10

1 Prepare the meat sauce and set aside. Butter a large shallow baking dish, preferably rectangular or square.

2 Make the béchamel sauce by gently heating the milk with the bay leaf and mace in a small saucepan. Melt the butter in a medium heavy saucepan. Add the flour, and mix it in well with a wire whisk. Cook for 2–3 minutes. Strain the hot milk into the flour and butter, and mix smoothly with the whisk. Bring the sauce to a boil, stirring constantly, and cook for 4–5 minutes more. Season with salt and pepper, and set aside.

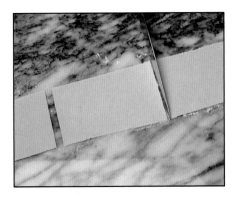

3 ▲ Make the pasta. Do not let it dry out before cutting it into rectangles approximately 4½ in wide and the same length as the baking dish (this will make it easier to assemble). Preheat the oven to 400°F.

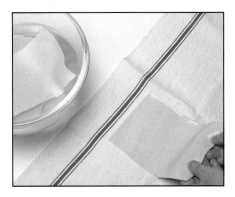

4 ▲ Bring a very large pan of water to a boil. Place a large bowl of cold water near the stove. Cover a large work surface with a tablecloth. Add salt to the rapidly boiling water. Drop in 3 or 4 of the egg pasta rectangles. Cook very briefly, about 30 seconds. Remove them from the pan using a slotted spoon, and drop them into the bowl of cold water for about 30 seconds. Pull them out of the water, shaking off the excess water. Lay them out flat without overlapping on the tablecloth. Continue with all the remaining pasta and trimmings.

5 ▲ To assemble the lasagne, have all the elements at hand: the baking dish, béchamel and meat sauces, pasta strips, grated Parmesan and butter. Spread one large spoonful of the meat sauce over the bottom of the dish. Arrange a layer of pasta in the dish, cutting it with a sharp knife so that it fits well inside the dish.

6 ▲ Cover with a thin layer of meat sauce, then one of béchamel. Sprinkle with a little cheese. Repeat the layers in the same order, ending with a layer of pasta coated with béchamel. Do not make more than about 6 layers of pasta. (If you have a lot left over, make another small lasagne in a little ovenproof dish.) Use the pasta trimmings to patch any gaps in the pasta. Sprinkle the top with Parmesan, and dot with butter.

7 Bake in the preheated oven for 20 minutes or until brown on top. Remove from the oven and allow to stand for 5 minutes before serving. Serve directly from the baking dish, cutting out rectangular or square sections for each helping.

~ VARIATION ~

If you are using dried or bought pasta, follow step 4, but boil the lasagne in just two batches, and stop the cooking about 4 minutes before the recommended cooking time on the package has elapsed. Rinse in cold water and lay the pasta out the same way as for the egg pasta.

Tortelli with Pumpkin Stuffing

Tortelli di zucca

During autumn and winter the northern Italian markets are full of bright orange pumpkins, which are used to make soups and pasta dishes. This dish is a speciality of Mantua.

Ingredients
2 lb pumpkin (weight with shell)
1½ cups amaretti cookies, crushed fine
2 eggs
¾ cup freshly grated Parmesan or
    Romano cheese
pinch of grated nutmeg
salt and freshly ground black pepper
plain breadcrumbs, as required
egg pasta sheets made with 3 eggs
To serve
½ cup butter
¾ cup freshly grated Parmesan or
    Romano cheese
serves 6–8

1 Preheat the oven to 375°. Cut the pumpkin into 4 in pieces. Leave the skin on. Place the pumpkin pieces in a covered casserole, and bake for 45–50 minutes. When cool, cut off the skins. Purée the flesh in a food mill or food processor or press through a sieve.

2 ▲ Combine the pumpkin purée with the cookie crumbs, eggs, cheese and nutmeg. Season with salt and pepper. If the mixture is too wet, add 1–2 tbsp of breadcrumbs. Set aside.

3 Prepare the sheets of egg pasta. Roll out very thinly by hand or machine. Do not let the pasta dry out before filling it.

4 ▲ Place tablespoons of filling every 2½ in along the pasta in rows 2 in apart. Cover with another sheet of pasta, and press down gently. Use a fluted pastry wheel to cut between the rows to form rectangles with filling in the center of each. Place the tortelli on a lightly floured surface, and allow to dry for at least 30 minutes. Turn them occasionally so they dry on both sides.

5 Bring a large pan of salted water to a boil. Gently heat the butter over very low heat, taking care that it does not darken.

6 ▲ Drop the tortelli into the boiling water. Stir to prevent from sticking. They will be cooked in 4–5 minutes. Drain and arrange in individual dishes. Spoon on the melted butter, sprinkle with Parmesan or Romano, and serve.

Fonduta with Steamed Vegetables

Fonduta con verdure

Fonduta is a creamy cheese sauce from the mountainous Val d'Aosta region. Traditionally it is garnished with slices of white truffles and eaten with toasted bread rounds.

Ingredients

assorted vegetables, such as fennel, broccoli, carrots, cauliflower and zucchini

½ cup butter

12–16 rounds of Italian or French baguette

For the fonduta

1⅔ cups fontina cheese

1 tbsp flour

milk, as required

¼ cup butter

½ cup freshly grated Parmesan or Romano cheese

pinch of grated nutmeg

salt and freshly ground black pepper

2 egg yolks, at room temperature

a few slivers of white truffle (optional)

serves 4

1 ▲ About 6 hours before you want to serve the fonduta, cut the fontina into chunks and place in a bowl. Sprinkle with the flour. Pour in enough milk to barely cover the cheese, and set aside in a cool place. If you put the bowl in the refrigerator, take it out at least 1 hour before cooking the fonduta. It should be at room temperature before being cooked.

2 Just before preparing the fonduta, steam the vegetables until tender. Cut into pieces. Place on a serving platter, dot with butter, and keep warm.

3 Butter the rounds and toast them lightly in the oven or the broiler.

4 ▲ For the fonduta, melt the butter in a mixing bowl set over a pan of simmering water, or in the top of a double boiler. Strain the fontina and add it, with 3–4 tbsp of its soaking milk. Cook, stirring, until the cheese melts. When it is hot, and has formed a homogenous mass, add the Parmesan or Romano and stir until melted. Season with nutmeg, salt and pepper.

5 ▲ Remove from the heat and immediately beat in the egg yolks which have been passed through a strainer. Spoon into warmed individual serving bowls, garnish with the white truffle if using, and serve with the vegetables and toasted bread.

Polenta

Polenta

Polenta is a form of cornmeal. It is eaten in northern Italy in place of rice or pasta.

Ingredients
6¼ cups water
1 tbsp salt
2½ cups polenta
serves 4–6

1 ▲ Bring the water to a boil in a large heavy saucepan. Add the salt. Reduce the heat to a simmer, and begin to add the polenta in a fine rain. Stir constantly with a whisk until the polenta has all been incorporated.

2 ▲ Switch to a long-handled wooden spoon, and continue to stir the polenta over low to moderate heat until it is a thick mass, and pulls away from the sides of the pan. This may take from 25–50 minutes, depending on the type of polenta used. For best results, never stop stirring the polenta until you remove it from the heat.

3 ▲ When the polenta is cooked, spoon it into a large slightly wet bowl, wait 5 minutes, and turn it out onto a serving platter. Serve it with a meat or tomato sauce, or follow the instructions given in the recipes on the following pages.

Fried Polenta

Polenta fritta

Leftover polenta can be fried, making a crispy appetizer to serve with drinks or antipasti.

Ingredients
cold leftover polenta
oil, for deep-frying
flour, for dredging
salt and freshly ground black pepper
serves 6–8 as an appetizer

2 Heat the oil until a small piece of bread sizzles as soon as it is dropped in (about 360°F).

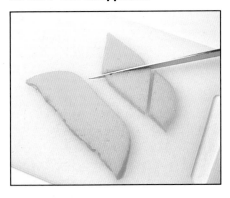

4 ▲ Fry the polenta, a few pieces at a time, until golden and crisp. Drain on paper towels while the remaining pieces are frying. Serve at once.

3 ▲ Season the flour with salt and pepper. Dredge the pieces lightly in the flour, shaking off any excess.

1 ▲ Cut the polenta into slices about ½ inch thick. Cut the slices into triangles or rounds.

Polenta with Mushrooms

Polenta con funghi

This dish is delicious made with a mixture of wild and cultivated mushrooms. Just a few dried porcini mushrooms will help to give cultivated mushrooms a more interesting flavor.

Ingredients

2 tbsp dried porcini mushrooms (omit if
　using wild mushrooms)
4 tbsp olive oil
1 small onion, finely chopped
1½ lb mushrooms, wild or cultivated, or a
　combination of both
2 cloves garlic, finely chopped
3 tbsp chopped fresh parsley
3 medium tomatoes, peeled and diced
1 tbsp tomato paste
¾ cup warm water
¼ tsp fresh thyme leaves, or ⅛ tsp
　dried thyme
1 bay leaf
salt and freshly ground black pepper
a few sprigs fresh parsley, to garnish

For the polenta

6¼ cups water
1 tbsp salt
2½ cups polenta

serves 6

3 ▲ Clean the fresh mushrooms by wiping them with a damp cloth. Cut into slices. When the onion is soft add the mushrooms to the pan. Stir over moderate to high heat until they give up their liquid. Add the garlic, parsley and diced tomatoes. Cook for 4–5 minutes more.

5 ▲ Bring the water to a boil in a large heavy saucepan. Add the salt. Reduce the heat to a simmer, and begin to add the polenta in a fine rain. Stir constantly with a whisk until the polenta has all been incorporated.

6 Switch to a long-handled wooden spoon, and continue to stir the polenta over low to moderate heat until it is a thick mass, and pulls away from the sides of the pan. This may take from 25–50 minutes, depending on the type of polenta used. For best results, never stop stirring the polenta until you remove it from the heat.

1 ▲ Soak the dried mushrooms, if using, in a small cup of warm water for 20 minutes. Remove the mushrooms with a slotted spoon, and rinse them well in several changes of cool water. Filter the soaking water through a layer of paper towels placed in a sieve, and reserve.

2 In a large frying pan heat the oil, and sauté the onion over low heat until soft and golden.

4 ▲ Soften the tomato paste in the warm water (use only ½ cup water if you are using dried mushrooms). Add it to the pan with the herbs. Add the dried mushrooms and soaking liquid, if using them. Mix well and season with salt and pepper. Lower the heat to low to moderate and cook for 15–20 minutes. Set aside while you make the polenta.

7 ▲ When the polenta has almost finished cooking, gently reheat the mushroom sauce. To serve, spoon the polenta onto a warmed serving platter. Make a well in the center. Spoon some of the mushroom sauce into the well, and garnish with parsley. Serve at once, passing the remaining sauce in a separate bowl.

Risotto with Cheese

Risotto alla parmigiana

Risotto is distinguished from other rice dishes by its unique cooking method.

Ingredients

5½ cups beef, chicken or vegetable
   stock, preferably home-made
5 tbsp butter
1 small onion, finely chopped
1½ cups medium-grain risotto rice, such
   as arborio
½ cup dry white wine
salt and freshly ground black pepper
¾ cup freshly grated Parmesan or
   Romano cheese

serves 3–4

1 Heat the stock in a medium saucepan, and keep it simmering until it is needed.

2 In a large heavy frying pan or casserole, melt two-thirds of the butter. Stir in the onion, and cook gently until it is soft and golden. Add the rice, mixing it well to coat it with butter. After 1–2 minutes pour in the wine.

3 ▲ Raise the heat slightly, and cook until the wine evaporates. Add one small ladleful of the hot stock. Over moderate heat cook until the stock is absorbed or evaporates, stirring the rice with a wooden spoon to prevent it from sticking to the pan. Add a little more stock, and stir until the rice dries out again. Continue stirring and adding the liquid a little at a time. After about 20 minutes of cooking time, taste the rice. Add salt and pepper.

4 Continue cooking, stirring and adding the liquid until the rice is *al dente*, or tender but still firm to the bite. The total cooking time of the risotto may be from 20–35 minutes. If you run out of stock, use hot water, but do not worry if the rice is done before you have used up all the stock.

5 ▲ Remove the risotto pan from the heat. Stir in the remaining butter and the cheese. Taste again for seasoning. Allow the risotto to rest for 3–4 minutes before serving.

Risotto with Shrimp

Risotto con gamberi

This shrimp risotto is given a soft pink color by the addition of a little tomato paste.

Ingredients

12 oz fresh shrimp in their shells
5 cups water
1 bay leaf
1–2 sprigs of parsley
1 tsp whole peppercorns
2 cloves garlic, peeled
5 tbsp butter
2 shallots, finely chopped
1½ cups medium-grain risotto rice, such
   as arborio
1 tbsp tomato paste softened in ½ cup
   dry white wine
salt and freshly ground black pepper

serves 4

1 Place the shrimp in a large saucepan with the water, herbs, peppercorns and garlic. Bring to a boil and cook for about 1 minute. Remove the shrimp, peel, and return the shells to the saucepan. Boil the shells for another 10 minutes. Strain. Return the broth to a saucepan, and simmer until needed.

2 Slice the shrimp in half lengthwise, removing the dark vein along the back. Set 4 halves aside for garnish, and roughly chop the rest.

3 Heat two-thirds of the butter in a casserole. Add the shallots and cook until golden. Stir in the shrimp. Cook for 1–2 minutes.

4 ▲ Add the rice, mixing well to coat it with butter. After 1–2 minutes pour in the tomato paste and wine. Follow steps 3–5 for Risotto with Cheese, omitting the cheese and garnishing with the reserved prawn halves.

Sole with Sweet and Sour Sauce

Sfogi in saor

This Venetian dish should be prepared 1–2 days before it is to be eaten.

Ingredients
3–4 fillets of sole, about 1¼ lb total,
    divided in half
4 tbsp flour
salt and freshly ground black pepper
pinch of ground cloves
6–8 tbsp olive oil
generous ¼ cup pine nuts
3 bay leaves
pinch of ground cinnamon
pinch of grated nutmeg
4 cloves
1 small onion, very finely sliced
¼ cup dry white wine
¼ cup white wine vinegar
⅓ cup sultanas
serves 4

1 Dredge the sole fillets in the flour seasoned with salt and pepper and the ground cloves.

2 Heat 3 tbsp of the oil in a heavy frying pan or skillet. Cook the sole fillets a few at a time until golden, about 3 minutes on each side. Add more oil as necessary.

3 ▲ Remove with a slotted spatula to a large shallow serving dish. Sprinkle with the pine nuts, bay leaves, cinnamon, nutmeg and whole cloves.

4 ▲ Heat the remaining oil in a saucepan. Add the onion, and cook over low heat until golden. Add the wine, vinegar and sultanas, and boil for 4–5 minutes. Pour over the fish. Cover the dish with foil, and leave in a cool place for 24–48 hours. Remove 2 hours before serving. This dish is traditionally eaten at room temperature.

Salt Cod with Parsley and Garlic

Baccalà alla bolognese

Salt cod is very popular all over Italy. For centuries it has been imported from Scandinavia. The very salty fish must be soaked for 24 hours in water to reduce its salt content.

Ingredients
1½ lb boneless and skinless salt cod,
    preferably in one piece
flour seasoned with freshly ground
    black pepper, for dredging
2 tbsp extra-virgin olive oil
3 tbsp finely chopped fresh parsley
2 cloves garlic, finely chopped
2 tbsp butter, cut into small pieces
lemon wedges, to serve
serves 4–5

1 Cut the salt cod into 2 in squares. Place them in a large bowl and cover with cold water. Allow to stand for at least 24 hours, changing the water frequently.

2 ▲ Preheat the oven to 375°F. Drain the fish, shaking out the excess moisture. Remove any remaining bones or skin. Dredge lightly in the seasoned flour.

3 Spread 1 tbsp of the oil over the bottom of a baking dish large enough to hold the fish in one layer.

4 ▲ Place the fish in the dish. Combine the chopped parsley and garlic, and sprinkle evenly over the fish. Sprinkle with the remaining oil, and dot with butter. Bake for 15 minutes. Turn the fish, and bake for 15–20 minutes more, or until tender. Serve at once, with the lemon wedges.

Roast Chicken with Fennel

Pollo con finocchio

In Italy this dish is prepared with wild fennel. Cultivated fennel bulb works just as well.

Ingredients
3½ lb roasting chicken
salt and freshly ground black pepper
1 onion, quartered
½ cup olive oil
2 medium fennel bulbs
1 clove garlic, peeled
pinch of grated nutmeg
3–4 thin slices pancetta or bacon
½ cup dry white wine
serves 4–5

1 Preheat the oven to 350°F. Rinse the chicken in cold water. Pat it dry inside and out with paper towels. Sprinkle the cavity with salt and pepper. Place the onion quarters in the cavity. Rub the chicken with about 3 tbsp of the olive oil. Place in a roasting pan.

2 Cut the green fronds from the tops of the fennel bulbs. Chop the fronds with the garlic. Place in a small bowl and mix with the nutmeg. Season with salt and pepper.

3 ▲ Sprinkle the fennel mixture over the chicken, pressing it onto the oiled skin. Cover the breast with the slices of pancetta or bacon. Sprinkle with 2 tbsp of oil. Place in the oven and roast for 30 minutes.

4 Meanwhile, boil or steam the fennel bulbs until barely tender. Remove from the heat and cut into quarters or sixths lengthwise. After the chicken has been cooking for 30 minutes, remove the pan from the oven. Baste the chicken with any oils in the pan.

5 Arrange the fennel pieces around the chicken. Sprinkle the fennel with the remaining oil. Pour about half the wine over the chicken, and return the pan to the oven.

6 ▲ After 30 minutes more, baste the chicken again. Pour on the remaining wine. Cook for 15–20 minutes more. To test, prick the thigh with a fork. If the juices run clear, the chicken is cooked. Transfer the chicken to a serving platter, and arrange the fennel around it.

Chicken with Ham and Cheese

Petti di pollo alla bolognese

This tasty combination comes from Emilia-Romagna, where it is also prepared with veal.

Ingredients
4 small chicken breasts, skinned and
   boned
flour seasoned with salt and freshly
   ground black pepper, for dredging
¼ cup butter
3–4 leaves fresh sage
4 thin slices prosciutto crudo, or cooked
   ham, cut in half
½ cup freshly grated Parmesan or
   Romano cheese
serves 4

1 Cut each breast in half lengthwise to make two flat fillets of approximately the same thickness. Dredge the chicken in the seasoned flour, and shake off the excess.

2 ▲ Preheat the broiler. Heat the butter in a large heavy frying pan or skillet with the sage leaves. Add the chicken in one layer, and cook over low to moderate heat until golden brown on both sides, turning as necessary.

3 ▲ Remove the chicken from the heat, and arrange on a flameproof serving dish or broiling pan. Place one piece of ham on each chicken fillet, and top with the grated Parmesan or Romano. Broil for 3–4 minutes, or until the cheese has melted.

Pork Braised in Milk with Carrots   *Lonza al latte con carote*

This method of slowly cooking a joint of pork produces a deliciously creamy gravy. It is a speciality of the Veneto region.

Ingredients

1½ lb lean loin of pork
3 tbsp olive oil
2 tbsp butter
1 small onion, finely chopped
1 stalk celery, finely chopped
8 carrots, cut into 2 in strips
2 bay leaves
1 tbsp peppercorns
salt, to taste
2 cups milk, scalded

serves 4–5

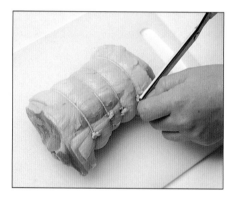

1 ▲ Trim any excess fat from the pork, and tie it into a roll with string.

2 ▲ Preheat the oven to 350°F. Heat the oil and butter in a large casserole. Add the vegetables, and cook over low heat until they soften, 8–10 minutes. Raise the heat, push the vegetables to one side and add the pork, browning it on all sides. Add the bay leaves and peppercorns, and season with salt.

3 ▲ Pour in the hot milk. Cover the casserole and place it in the center of the oven. Bake for about 90 minutes, turning and basting the pork with the sauce about once every 20 minutes. Remove the cover for the last 20 minutes of baking.

4 ▲ Remove the meat from the casserole, and cut off the string. Place the meat on a warmed serving platter and cut into slices.

~ VARIATION ~

This dish can also be made using a joint of veal. Substitute a piece of boneless veal and proceed as in the recipe. This dish is delicious served hot or cold.

5 ▲ Discard the bay leaves. Press about one-third of the carrots and all the liquids in the pan through a strainer. Arrange the remaining carrots around the meat.

6 ▲ Place the sauce in a small saucepan, taste for seasoning, and bring to a boil. If it seems too thin, boil it for a few minutes to reduce it slightly. Serve the sliced meat with the carrots, and pass the hot sauce separately.

Liver with Onions

Fegato alla veneziana

This classic Venetian dish is very good served with grilled polenta. Allow enough time for the onions to cook very slowly, to produce a sweet flavor.

Ingredients

⅓ cup butter
3 tbsp olive oil
1½ lb onions, very finely sliced
salt and freshly ground black pepper
1¾ lb calfs liver, sliced thinly
3 tbsp finely chopped fresh parsley, to garnish
grilled polenta wedges, to serve (optional)
serves 6

1 ▲ Heat two-thirds of the butter with the oil in a large heavy frying pan. Add the onions, and cook over low heat until soft and tender, about 40–50 minutes, stirring often. Season with salt and pepper. Remove to a side dish.

2 ▲ Heat the remaining butter in the pan over moderate to high heat. When it has stopped bubbling add the liver, and brown it on both sides. Cook for about 5 minutes, or until done. Remove to a warmed side dish.

3 ▲ Return the onions to the pan. Raise the heat slightly, and stir the onions to mix them into the liver cooking juices.

4 ▲ When the onions are hot, turn them out onto a heated serving platter. Arrange the liver on top, and sprinkle with parsley. Serve with grilled polenta wedges, if desired.

Rabbit with Tomatoes

Coniglio con pomodori

Rabbit is very popular in Italy, and is prepared in many ways. This is a hearty dish with strong and robust flavors.

Ingredients

1½ lb boned rabbit, cut into chunks
2 cloves garlic, thinly sliced
½ cup thinly sliced pancetta or lean bacon
1½ lb tomatoes, peeled, seeded and
    roughly chopped
3 tbsp chopped fresh basil
salt and freshly ground black pepper
4 tbsp olive oil

serves 4–5

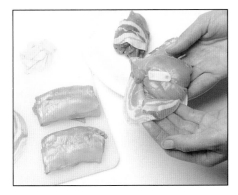

1 ▲ Preheat the oven to 400°F. Pat the rabbit pieces dry with paper towels. Place a thin slice of garlic on each piece. Wrap a slice of pancetta or bacon around it, making sure the garlic is held in place.

2 ▲ Place the tomatoes in a non-stick pan, and cook them for a few minutes until they give up some of their liquid and begin to dry out. Stir in the basil, and season with salt and pepper.

3 ▲ Place the tomatoes in a layer in the bottom of a baking dish. Arrange the rabbit pieces on top of the tomatoes. Sprinkle with olive oil and place, uncovered, in the oven. Roast for 40–50 minutes.

4 ▲ Baste the rabbit occasionally with any fat in the dish. After the rabbit has cooked for about 25 minutes the dish may be covered with foil for the remaining time if the sauce seems to be too dry.

Italian Bread Sticks
Grissini

These typically Italian bread sticks are especially delicious when hand-made. They are still sold loose in many bakeries in Turin and the north of Italy.

Ingredients
1 tbsp fresh cake yeast or ⅓ package
    active dried yeast
½ cup lukewarm water
pinch of sugar
2 tsp malt extract (optional)
1 tsp salt
1¾–2 cups white unbleached flour
makes about 30

1 ▲ Warm a medium mixing bowl by swirling some hot water in it. Drain. Place the yeast in the bowl, and pour on the warm water. Stir in the sugar, mix with a fork, and allow to stand until the yeast has dissolved and starts to foam, 5–10 minutes.

2 ▲ Use a wooden spoon to mix in the malt extract, if using, the salt and about one-third of the flour. Mix in another third of the flour, stirring with the spoon until the dough forms a mass and begins to pull away from the sides of the bowl.

3 ▲ Sprinkle some of the remaining flour onto a smooth work surface. Remove all of the dough from the bowl, and begin to knead it, working in the remaining flour a little at a time. Knead for 8–10 minutes. By the end the dough should be elastic and smooth. Form it into a ball.

4 ▲ Tear a lump the size of a small walnut from the ball of dough. Roll it lightly between your hands into a small sausage shape. Set it aside on a lightly floured surface. Repeat until all the dough is used up. There should be about 30 pieces.

~ VARIATION ~

Grissini are also good when rolled lightly in poppy or sesame seeds before being baked.

5 ▲ Place one piece of dough on a clean smooth work surface without any flour on it. Roll the dough under the spread-out fingers of both hands, moving your hands backwards and forwards to lengthen and thin the dough into a long strand about ⅜ inch thick. Transfer to a very lightly greased cookie sheet. Repeat with the remaining dough pieces, taking care to roll all the grissini to about the same thickness.

6 ▲ Preheat the oven to 400°F. Cover the tray with a cloth, and place the grissini in a warm place to rise for 10–15 minutes while the oven is heating. Bake for about 8–10 minutes. Remove from the oven. Turn the grissini over, and return them to the oven for 6–7 minutes more. Do not let them brown. Allow to cool. Grissini should be crisp when served. If they lose their crispness on a damp day, warm them in a moderate oven for a few minutes before serving.

Italian Coffee Dessert

Tiramisù

"Tiramisù" means "pick me up", and this rich egg and coffee dessert does just that!

Ingredients
1 lb 2 oz mascarpone cheese
5 eggs, separated, at room temperature
scant ½ cup superfine sugar
pinch of salt
lady fingers or slices of sponge cake, to line dish(es)
½ cup strong Italian espresso coffee
4 tbsp brandy or rum (optional)
unsweetened cocoa powder, to sprinkle
serves 6–8

1 Beat the mascarpone in a small bowl until soft. In a separate bowl beat the egg yolks with the sugar (reserving 1 tbsp) until the mixture is pale yellow and fluffy. Gradually beat in the softened mascarpone.

2 ▲ Using an electric beater or wire whisk, beat the egg whites with the salt until they form stiff peaks. Fold the egg whites into the mascarpone mixture.

3 Line one large or several individual serving dishes with the cookies or cake slices. Add the reserved sugar to the coffee, and stir in the liqueur.

4 ▲ Sprinkle the coffee over the cookies. They should be moist but not saturated. Cover with half of the egg mixture. Make another layer of cookies moistened with coffee, and cover with the remaining egg mixture. Sprinkle with cocoa powder. Refrigerate for at least 1 hour, preferably more, before serving.

Italian Custard

Zabaione

This airy egg custard fortified with sweet wine is most often eaten warm with cookies or fruit.

Ingredients
3 egg yolks
3 tbsp sugar
5 tbsp marsala or white dessert wine
pinch of grated orange zest
serves 3–4

1 ▲ In the top half of a double boiler, or in a bowl, away from the heat, whisk the egg yolks with the sugar until pale yellow. Beat in the marsala or wine.

2 ▲ Place the pan or bowl over a pan of simmering water, and continue whisking until the custard is a frothy, light mass and evenly coats the back of a spoon, 6–8 minutes. Do not let the upper container touch the hot water, or the zabaione may curdle.

3 ▲ Stir in the orange zest. Serve immediately.

~ COOK'S TIP ~

A small teaspoon of ground cinnamon may be added to the zabalone.

CENTRAL ITALY

The six regions which comprise Central Italy – Tuscany; Umbria; Marches; Lazio; Abruzzo, and Molise – have discovered relative comfort in recent years. Rome, Florence and Siena capture a huge proportion of the tourism: and the Central regions, positioned between the poor South and the industrial North, are well placed to profit most when Italy has success.

This well-being is reflected in the cuisine. Still drawing from a peasant heritage, many dishes are interpreted in a slightly more sophisticated style. Ingredients are a little more elaborate and expensive, and their much broader range also reflects the wide-reaching and varied geography of the region.

Broccoli Soup

Zuppa di broccoletti

Around Rome broccoli grows abundantly and is served in this soup with garlic toasts.

Ingredients
1½ lb broccoli spears
7½ cups fresh or canned chicken or
   vegetable stock
salt and freshly ground black pepper
1 tbsp fresh lemon juice
To serve
6 slices white bread
1 large clove garlic, cut in half
freshly grated Parmesan cheese, to serve
   (optional)
serves 6

1 Using a small sharp knife, peel the broccoli stems, starting from the base of the stalks and pulling gently up towards the florets. (The peel comes off very easily.) Chop the broccoli into small chunks.

2 Bring the stock to a boil in a large saucepan. Add the broccoli and simmer for 30 minutes, or until soft.

3 ▲ Purée about half of the soup and mix into the rest of the soup. Season with salt, pepper and lemon juice.

4 ▲ Just before serving, reheat the soup to just below boiling point. Toast the bread, rub with garlic and cut into quarters. Place 3 or 4 pieces of toast in the bottom of each soup plate. Ladle on the soup. Serve at once, with Parmesan if desired.

Tomato and Bread Soup

Pappa al pomodoro

This colorful Florentine recipe was created to use up stale bread. It can be made with very ripe fresh or canned plum tomatoes.

Ingredients
6 tbsp olive oil
small piece of dried chili, crumbled
   (optional)
1½ cups stale coarse white bread, cut
   into 1 in cubes
1 medium onion, finely chopped
2 cloves garlic, finely chopped
1½ lb ripe tomatoes, peeled and
   chopped, or 2 × 14 oz cans peeled
   plum tomatoes, chopped
3 tbsp chopped fresh basil
6¼ cups fresh or canned stock or water,
   or a combination of both
salt and freshly ground black pepper
extra-virgin olive oil, to serve (optional)
serves 4

1 Heat 4 tbsp of the oil in a large saucepan. Add the chili, if using, and stir for 1–2 minutes. Add the bread cubes and cook until golden. Remove to a plate and drain on paper towels.

2 ▲ Add the remaining oil, the onion and garlic, and cook until the onion softens. Stir in the tomatoes, bread and basil. Season with salt. Cook over moderate heat, stirring occasionally, for about 15 minutes.

3 Meanwhile, heat the stock or water to simmering. Add it to the saucepan with the tomato mixture, and mix well. Bring to a boil. Lower the heat slightly and simmer for 20 minutes.

4 ▲ Remove the soup from the heat. Use a fork to mash the tomatoes and the bread together. Season with pepper, and more salt if necessary. Allow to stand for 10 minutes. Just before serving swirl in a little extra-virgin olive oil, if desired.

White Bean Soup

Minestrone di fagioli

A thick purée of cooked dried beans is at the heart of this substantial country soup from Tuscany. It makes a warming winter lunch or supper dish.

Ingredients

1½ cups dried cannellini or other white beans
1 bay leaf
5 tbsp olive oil
1 medium onion, finely chopped
1 carrot, finely chopped
1 stalk celery, finely chopped
3 medium tomatoes, peeled and finely chopped
2 cloves garlic, finely chopped
1 tsp fresh thyme leaves, or ½ tsp dried thyme
3½ cups boiling water
salt and freshly ground black pepper
extra-virgin olive oil, to serve
serves 6

1 ▲ Pick over the beans carefully, discarding any stones or other particles. Soak the beans in a large bowl of cold water overnight. Drain. Place the beans in a large saucepan of water, bring to a boil, and cook for 20 minutes. Drain. Return the beans to the pan, cover with cold water, and bring to a boil again. Add the bay leaf, and cook until the beans are tender, 1–2 hours. Drain again. Remove the bay leaf.

2 Purée about three-quarters of the beans in a food processor, or pass through a food mill, adding a little water if necessary.

3 Heat the oil in a large saucepan. Stir in the onion, and cook until it softens. Add the carrot and celery, and cook for 5 minutes more.

4 ▲ Stir in the tomatoes, garlic and thyme. Cook for 6–8 minutes more, stirring often.

5 ▲ Pour in the boiling water. Stir in the beans and the bean purée. Season with salt and pepper. Simmer for 10–15 minutes. Serve in individual soup bowls, sprinkled with a little extra-virgin olive oil.

Pasta and Lentil Soup

Pasta e lenticchie

The small brown lentils which are grown in central Italy are usually used in this wholesome soup, but green lentils may be substituted if preferred.

Ingredients

1 cup dried green or brown lentils, picked over
6 tbsp olive oil
¼ cup ham or salt pork, cut into small dice
1 medium onion, finely chopped
1 stalk celery, finely chopped
1 carrot, finely chopped
9 cups chicken stock or water, or a combination of both
1 leaf fresh sage or ⅛ tsp dried sage
1 sprig fresh thyme or ¼ tsp dried thyme
salt and freshly ground black pepper
2½ cups ditalini, pastina, or other small soup pasta

serves 4–6

1 ▲ Carefully check the lentils for small pitts. Place them in a bowl, covered with cold water, and soak for 2–3 hours. Rinse and drain well.

2 ▲ In a large saucepan, heat the oil and sauté the ham or salt pork for 2–3 minutes. Add the onion, and cook gently until it softens.

3 ▲ Stir in the celery and carrot, and cook for 5 minutes more, stirring frequently. Add the lentils, and stir to coat them in the fats.

4 ▲ Pour in the stock or water and the herbs, and bring the soup to a boil. Cook over moderate heat for about 1 hour or until the lentils are tender. Add salt and pepper to taste.

5 Stir in the pasta, and cook it until it is just done. Allow the soup to stand for a few minutes before serving.

Tuscan Baked Beans

Fagioli al forno alla toscana

Beans, both dried and fresh, are particularly popular in Tuscany, where they are cooked in many different ways. In this vegetarian dish the beans are flavored with fresh sage leaves.

Ingredients

1 lb 6 oz dried beans, such as cannellini
4 tbsp olive oil
2 cloves garlic, crushed
3 leaves fresh sage (if fresh sage is not available use 4 tbsp chopped fresh parsley)
1 leek, finely sliced
1 × 14 oz can plum tomatoes, chopped, with their juice
salt and freshly ground black pepper
serves 6–8

3 ▲ In a large deep baking dish combine the beans with the leek and tomatoes. Stir in the oil with the garlic and sage. Add enough fresh water to cover the beans by 1 inch. Mix well. Cover the dish with a lid or foil, and place in the center of the preheated oven. Bake for 1¾ hours.

4 ▲ Remove the dish from the oven, stir the beans, and season with salt and pepper. Return the beans to the oven, uncovered, and cook for another 15 minutes, or until the beans are tender. Remove from the oven and allow to stand for 7–8 minutes before serving. Serve hot or at room temperature.

1 ▲ Carefully pick over the beans, discarding any stones or other particles. Place the beans in a large bowl and cover with water. Soak for at least 6 hours, or overnight. Drain.

2 ▲ Preheat the oven to 350°F. In a small saucepan heat the oil and sauté the garlic cloves and sage leaves for 3–4 minutes until garlic is tender but not brown. Remove from the heat.

Egg and Cheese Soup

Stracciatella

In this classic Roman soup, eggs and cheese are beaten into hot broth, producing a slightly 'stringy' texture characteristic of the dish.

Ingredients

3 eggs
3 tbsp fine semolina
6 tbsp freshly grated Parmesan cheese
pinch of nutmeg
6¼ cups fresh or canned beef or chicken
 stock
salt and freshly ground black pepper
12 rounds of French bread, to serve
serves 6

3 ▲ When the stock is hot, and a few minutes before you are ready to serve the soup, whisk the egg mixture into the broth. Raise the heat slightly, and bring it barely to a boil. Season with salt and pepper. Cook for 3–4 minutes. As the egg cooks, the soup will not be completely smooth.

4 ▲ To serve, toast the rounds of French bread and place 2 in the bottom of each soup plate. Ladle on the hot soup, and serve immediately.

1 ▲ Beat the eggs in a bowl with the semolina and the cheese. Add the nutmeg. Beat in 1 cupful of the cool stock.

2 ▲ Meanwhile heat the remaining stock to simmering point in a large saucepan.

Broad Bean Purée with Ham

Purea di fave con prosciutto

Peeling broad beans leaves them tender and sweet. They go particularly well with the saltiness of prosciutto crudo in this Tuscan combination.

Ingredients
2 lb fresh broad beans in their pods, or
   14 oz shelled broad beans, thawed if
   frozen
1 medium onion, finely chopped
2 small potatoes, peeled and diced
¼ cup prosciutto crudo
3 tbsp extra-virgin olive oil
salt and freshly ground black pepper
serves 4

1 Place the shelled beans in a saucepan and cover with water. Bring to a boil and cook for 5 minutes. Drain. When they are cool enough to handle, peel the beans.

2 ▲ Place the peeled beans in a saucepan with the onion and potatoes. Add enough water just to cover the vegetables. Bring to a boil. Lower the heat slightly, cover, and simmer until the vegetables are very soft, 15–20 minutes. Check occasionally that all the water has not evaporated. If necessary add a few tablespoons more.

3 Chop the ham into very small dice. Heat the oil and sauté until the ham is just golden.

4 ▲ Mash or purée the bean mixture. Return it to the pan. If it is very moist, cook it over moderate heat until it reduces slightly. Stir in the oil with the ham. Season and cook for 2 minutes.

Deep-fried Cauliflower

Cavolfiore fritto

Deep-frying is very popular in Italy, and everything from cheese to fruit may be fried. The cauliflower may be eaten as a side dish or as an antipasto.

Ingredients
1 large cauliflower
1 egg
salt and freshly ground black pepper
scant 1 cup flour
¾ cup dry white wine
oil, for deep-frying
serves 4

1 Soak the cauliflower in a bowl of salted water. In a mixing bowl, beat the egg. Season and beat in the flour. The mixture will be very thick. Add the wine. If necessary add more to make a fairly runny batter. Cover, and allow to rest for 30 minutes.

2 Steam or boil the cauliflower until just tender – do not overcook. Cut it into small florets when cool.

3 ▲ Heat the oil until a small piece of bread sizzles as soon as it is dropped in (about 360°F). Dip each cauliflower piece into the batter before deep-frying it until golden.

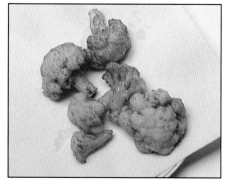

4 ▲ Remove from the oil with a slotted spoon and drain on paper towels. Sprinkle lightly with salt and serve hot.

Aromatic Stewed Mushrooms

Funghi trifolati

This dish from Piedmont combines both field and cultivated mushrooms, which give a balanced but not overwhelming flavor.

Ingredients
1½ lb firm fresh mushrooms, field and
    cultivated
6 tbsp olive oil
2 cloves garlic, finely chopped
salt and freshly ground black pepper
3 tbsp chopped fresh parsley
serves 6

2 ▲ Cut off the woody tips of the stems and discard. Slice the stems and caps fairly thickly.

3 ▲ Heat the oil in a large frying pan. Stir in the garlic and, after about 1 minute, the mushrooms. Cook for 8–10 minutes, stirring occasionally. Season with salt and pepper, and stir in the parsley. Cook for 5 minutes more, and serve at once.

1 ▲ Clean the mushrooms carefully by wiping them with a damp cloth or paper towels.

Sautéed Peas with Ham

Piselli alla fiorentina

When fresh peas are in season, they can be stewed with a little ham and onion and served as a substantial side dish.

Ingredients
3 tbsp olive oil
½ cup pancetta or ham, finely diced
3 tbsp finely chopped onion
2 lb whole peas (about 11 oz shelled) or
    10 oz frozen petit pois, thawed
2–3 tbsp water
salt and freshly ground black pepper
a few leaves fresh mint or sprigs parsley
additional parsley or mint to garnish
    (optional)
serves 4

1 Heat the oil in a medium saucepan, and sauté the pancetta or ham and onion for 2–3 minutes.

2 ▲ Stir in the shelled fresh or thawed frozen peas. Add the water. Season with salt and pepper and mix well to coat with the oil.

3 ▲ Add the fresh herbs, cover, and cook over moderate heat until tender. This may take from 5 minutes for sweet fresh peas, to 15 for tougher, older peas. Serve as a side dish to meat dishes or frittate.

Carpaccio with Arugula

Carpaccio con rucola

Carpaccio is a fine dish of raw beef marinated in lemon juice and olive oil. It is traditionally served with flakes of fresh Parmesan cheese. Use very fresh meat of the best quality.

Ingredients
1 clove of garlic, peeled and cut in half
1½ lemons
¼ cup extra-virgin olive oil
salt and freshly ground black pepper
2 bunches arugula
4 very thin slices of beef top round
1 cup Parmesan cheese, thinly
    shaved
serves 4

1 Rub a small bowl all over with the cut side of the garlic. Squeeze the lemons into the bowl. Whisk in the olive oil. Season with salt and pepper. Allow the sauce to stand for at least 15 minutes before using.

2 ▲ Carefully wash the arugula and tear off any thick stalks. Spin or pat dry. Arrange the arugula around the edge of a serving platter, or divide on 4 individual plates.

3 ▲ Place the beef in the center of the platter, and pour on the sauce, spreading it evenly over the meat. Arrange the shaved Parmesan on top of the meat slices. Serve at once.

Tuna in Rolled Red Peppers

Peperoni rossi ripieni di tonno

This savory combination originated in southern Italy. Grilled peppers have a sweet, smoky taste that combines particularly well with fish.

Ingredients
3 large red peppers
1 × 7 oz can tuna fish, drained
2 tbsp fresh lemon juice
3 tbsp olive oil
6 green or black olives, pitted and
    chopped
2 tbsp chopped fresh parsley
1 clove garlic, finely chopped
1 medium stalk celery, very finely
    chopped
salt and freshly ground black pepper
serves 4–6

1 Place the peppers under a hot broiler, and turn occasionally until they are black and blistered on all sides. Remove from the heat and place in a paper bag.

2 ▲ Leave for 5 minutes, and then peel. Cut the peppers into quarters, and remove the stems and seeds.

3 Meanwhile, flake the tuna and combine with the lemon juice and oil. Stir in the remaining ingredients. Season with salt and pepper.

4 ▲ Lay the pepper segments out flat, skin side down. Divide the tuna mixture equally between them. Spread it out, pressing it into an even layer. Roll the peppers up. Place the pepper rolls in the refrigerator for at least 1 hour. Just before serving, cut each roll in half with a sharp knife.

Fried Rice Balls Stuffed with Cheese

Supplì

These deep-fried balls of risotto are stuffed with an inner filling of mozzarella cheese. They are very popular snacks in Rome and central Italy.

Ingredients

1 recipe Risotto with Parmesan Cheese
    or Risotto with Mushrooms
3 eggs
⅔ cup mozzarella cheese, cut into small
    dice
oil, for deep-frying
plain breadcrumbs, as required
flour, to coat
serves 4

1 ▲ Allow the risotto to cool completely. (These are even better when formed from risotto made the day before.) Beat 2 of the eggs, and mix them well into the cold risotto.

2 ▲ Use your hands to form the rice mixture into balls the size of a large egg. If the mixture is too moist to hold its shape well, stir in a few tablespoons of breadcrumbs as necessary. Poke a hole into the center of each ball, fill it with a few small cubes of mozzarella, and close the hole over again with the rice mixture.

3 Heat the oil until a small piece of bread sizzles as soon as it is dropped in (about 360°F).

4 ▲ Spread some flour on a plate. Beat the remaining egg in a shallow bowl. Sprinkle another plate with breadcrumbs. Roll the balls in the flour, then in the egg, and finally in the breadcrumbs.

5 ▲ Fry them a few at a time in the hot oil until golden and crisp. Drain on paper towels while the remaining balls are frying. Serve hot.

Semolina Gnocchi

Gnocchi di semola

This famous Roman dish is made with coarsely ground semolina, which is cooked in a similar way to polenta. The rich paste is cut into flat discs, and baked with butter and cheese.

Ingredients

4½ cups milk
pinch of salt
3 tbsp butter
generous 2 cups coarsely ground
    semolina
3 egg yolks
3 tbsp freshly grated Parmesan or
    Romano cheese

For baking

5 tbsp butter, melted
½ cup freshly grated Parmesan or
    Romano cheese
pinch of grated nutmeg

serves 4

1 ▲ Heat the milk with the salt and a third of the butter in a heavy or non-stick saucepan. When it boils sprinkle in the semolina, stirring with a wire whisk to prevent lumps from forming. Bring the mixture to a boil. Lower heat and simmer for 15–20 minutes, stirring occasionally. The mixture will be very thick.

2 ▲ Remove from the heat and beat in the remaining butter, and then the egg yolks one at a time. Stir in the grated Parmesan or Romano. Season with salt. Sprinkle a little cold water onto a work surface. Spread the hot semolina mixture out onto it in an even layer about ½ inch thick. Allow to cool for at least 2 hours.

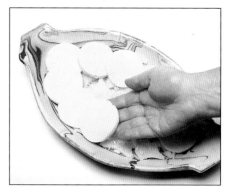

4 ▲ Place the trimmings in an even layer in the bottom of the dish. Pour over a little melted butter, and sprinkle with cheese. Cover with a layer of the cut-out circles, overlapping them slightly. Sprinkle with nutmeg, cheese and butter. Continue the layering until all the ingredients have been used up.

~ COOK'S TIP ~

Semolina is ground durum wheat, which is the kind used to make dried pasta. Buy semolina in small batches and store in an air-tight container as it goes stale when kept for too long.

3 ▲ Preheat the oven to 425°F. Butter a shallow baking dish. Use a biscuit cutter to cut the semolina into 2½ in rounds.

5 Bake for about 20 minutes, or until the top is browned. Remove from the oven and allow to stand for 5 minutes before serving.

Penne with Tuna and Mozzarella *Penne con tonno e mozzarella*

This tasty sauce is quickly made from kitchen cupboard staples, with the addition of fresh mozzarella. If possible, use tuna canned in olive oil.

Ingredients
1 lb penne, or other short pasta
1 tbsp capers, in brine or salt
2 cloves garlic
3 tbsp chopped fresh parsley
1 × 7 oz can of tuna, drained
5 tbsp olive oil
salt and freshly ground black pepper
⅔ cup mozzarella cheese, cut into
    small dice
serves 4

1 Bring a large pan of salted water to a boil and drop in the pasta.

2 ▲ Rinse the capers well in water. Chop them finely with the garlic. Combine with the parsley and the tuna. Stir in the oil, and season with salt and pepper, if necessary.

3 ▲ Drain the pasta when it is just *al dente*. Tip it into a large frying pan. Add the tuna sauce and the diced mozzarella, and cook over moderate heat, stirring constantly, until the cheese just begins to melt. Serve at once.

Spaghettini with Vodka and Caviar *Spaghettini con vodka e caviale*

This is an elegant yet easy way to serve spaghettini. In Rome it is an after-theater favorite.

Ingredients
4 tbsp olive oil
3 scallions, thinly sliced
1 clove garlic, finely chopped
½ cup vodka
⅔ cup heavy cream
½ cup black or red caviar
salt and freshly ground black pepper
1 lb spaghettini
serves 4

1 ▲ Heat the oil in a small frying pan. Add the scallions and garlic, and cook gently for 4–5 minutes.

2 ▲ Add the vodka and cream, and cook over low heat for about 5–8 minutes more.

~ COOK'S TIP ~

The finest caviar is salted sturgeon roe. Red "caviar" is salmon roe, cheaper and often saltier than sturgeon roe, as is the black-dyed lump fish roe.

3 ▲ Remove from the heat and stir in the caviar. Season with salt and pepper as necessary.

4 Meanwhile, cook the spaghettini in a large pan of rapidly boiling salted water until *al dente*. Drain the pasta, and toss immediately with the sauce.

Short Pasta with Cauliflower   *Pennoni rigati con cavolfiore*

This is a pasta version of cauliflower cheese. The cauliflower water is used to boil the pasta.

Ingredients

1 medium cauliflower
2 cups milk
1 bay leaf
¼ cup butter
½ cup flour
salt and freshly ground black pepper
¾ cup freshly grated Parmesan or
   Romano cheese
1¼ lb pennoni rigati, tortiglioni, or other
   short pasta

serves 6

1 Bring a large pan of water to a boil. Wash the cauliflower well, and separate it into florets. Boil the florets until they are just tender, about 8–10 minutes. Remove them from the pan with a strainer or slotted spoon. Chop the cauliflower into bite-size pieces and set aside. Do not discard the cooking water.

2 ▲ Make a béchamel sauce by gently heating the milk with the bay leaf in a small saucepan. Do not let it boil. Melt the butter in a medium heavy saucepan. Add the flour, and mix it in well with a wire whisk ensuring there are no lumps. Cook for 2–3 minutes, but do not let the butter burn.

3 Strain the hot milk into the flour and butter mixture all at once, and mix smoothly with the whisk.

4 Bring the sauce to a boil, stirring constantly, and cook for 4–5 minutes more. Season with salt and pepper. Add the cheese, and stir over low heat until it melts. Stir in the cauliflower.

5 ▲ Bring the cooking water back to a boil. Add salt, and stir in the pasta. Cook until it is *al dente*. Drain, and tip the pasta into a warm serving bowl. Pour over the sauce. Mix well, and serve at once.

Spaghetti with Bacon and Onion   *Spaghetti all'amatriciana*

This easy sauce is quickly made from ingredients that are almost always at hand.

Ingredients

2 tbsp olive oil
½ cup unsmoked lean bacon, cut into
   matchsticks
1 small onion, finely chopped
½ cup dry white wine
1 lb tomatoes, fresh or canned, chopped
¼ tsp thyme leaves
salt and freshly ground black pepper
1¼ lb spaghetti
freshly grated Parmesan cheese, to serve

serves 6

1 In a medium frying pan, heat the oil. Add the bacon and onion, and cook over low to moderate heat until the onion is golden and the bacon has rendered its fat and is beginning to brown, about 8–10 minutes. Bring a large pan of water to a boil.

2 ▲ Add the wine to the bacon and onion, raise the heat, and cook rapidly until the liquid boils off. Add the tomatoes, thyme, salt and pepper. Cover, and cook over moderate heat for 10–15 minutes.

3 ▲ Meanwhile, add salt to the boiling water, and cook the pasta until it is *al dente*. Drain, toss with the sauce, and serve with the grated Parmesan.

Fettuccine with Ham and Cream *Fettuccine con prosciutto*

Prosciutto is perfect for this rich and delicious dish, which makes an elegant first course.

Ingredients
1 × 4 oz slice prosciutto crudo or other
    unsmoked ham
¼ cup butter
2 shallots, very finely chopped
salt and freshly ground black pepper
¾ cup heavy cream
12 oz fettuccine
½ cup grated Parmesan cheese
sprig fresh parsley, to garnish
serves 4

1 ▲ Cut the fat from the ham, and chop both lean and fat parts separately into small squares.

2 ▲ Melt the butter in a medium frying pan, and add the shallots and the squares of ham fat. Cook until golden. Add the lean ham, and cook for 2 minutes more. Season with black pepper. Stir in the cream, and keep warm over low heat while the pasta is cooking.

3 ▲ Boil the pasta in a large pan of rapidly boiling salted water. Drain when *al dente*. Turn into a warmed serving bowl, and toss with the sauce. Stir in the cheese and serve at once, garnished with a sprig of parsley.

~ VARIATION ~

Substitute 6 oz fresh or frozen peas for the ham. Add to the pan with the shallots.

Tagliatelle with Smoked Salmon *Tagliatelle con salmone affumicato*

In Italy smoked salmon is imported, and quite expensive. This elegant creamy sauce makes a little go a long way. Use a mixture of green and white pasta if you wish.

Ingredients
¾ cup smoked salmon slices or ends,
    fresh or frozen
1¼ cups light cream
pinch of ground mace or nutmeg
12 oz green and white tagliatelle
salt and freshly ground black pepper
3 tbsp chopped fresh chives, to garnish
serves 4–5

1 Cut the salmon into thin strips about 2 in long. Place in a bowl with the cream and the mace or nutmeg. Stir, cover, and allow to stand for at least 2 hours in a cool place.

2 ▲ Bring a large pan of water to a boil for the pasta. While the water is heating, gently warm the cream and salmon mixture in a small saucepan without boiling it.

3 ▲ Add salt to the boiling water. Drop in the pasta all at once. Drain when it is just *al dente*. Pour the sauce over the pasta and mix well. Season and garnish with the chives.

Spaghetti with Garlic and Oil

Spaghetti con aglio e olio

This is one of the simplest and most satisfying pasta dishes of all. It is very popular throughout Italy. Use the best quality oil available for this dish.

Ingredients

1 lb spaghetti
6 tbsp extra-virgin olive oil
3 cloves garlic, chopped
4 tbsp chopped fresh parsley
salt and freshly ground black pepper
freshly grated Parmesan cheese, to serve
   (optional)
serves 4

1 Drop the spaghetti into a large pan of rapidly boiling salted water.

2 ▲ In a large frying pan heat the oil and gently sauté the garlic until it is barely golden. Do not let it brown or it will taste bitter. Stir in the parsley. Season with salt and pepper. Remove from the heat until the pasta is ready.

3 ▲ Drain the pasta when it is barely *al dente*. Tip it into the pan with the oil and garlic, and cook together for 2–3 minutes, stirring well to coat the spaghetti with the sauce. Serve at once in a warmed serving bowl, with Parmesan, if desired.

Spaghetti with Walnut Sauce

Spaghetti con salsa di noci

Like pesto, this sauce is traditionally ground in a mortar and pestle, but works just as well made in a food processor. It is also very good on tagliatelle and other noodles.

Ingredients

1 cup walnut pieces or halves
3 tbsp plain breadcrumbs
3 tbsp olive or walnut oil
3 tbsp chopped fresh parsley
1–2 cloves garlic (optional)
¼ cup butter, at room temperature
2 tbsp cream
salt and freshly ground black pepper
14 oz whole wheat spaghetti
freshly grated Parmesan cheese, to serve
serves 4

1 Drop the nuts into a small pan of boiling water, and cook for 1–2 minutes. Drain. Slip off the skins. Dry on paper towels. Coarsely chop and set aside about a quarter of the nuts.

2 ▲ Place the remaining nuts, the breadcrumbs, oil, parsley and garlic, if using, in a food processor or blender. Process to a paste. Remove to a bowl, and stir in the softened butter and the cream. Season with salt and pepper.

3 ▲ Cook the pasta in a large pan of rapidly boiling salted water until *al dente*. Drain, and toss with the sauce. Sprinkle with the reserved chopped nuts, and pass the Parmesan separately.

Bread with Grapes

Schiacciata con uva

This bread is made to celebrate the grape harvest in central Italy. Use small black grapes with or without seeds; in Italy wine grapes are used.

Ingredients

1½ lb small black grapes
½ cup sugar
1 recipe Basic Pizza Dough, risen once
2 tbsp olive oil
serves 6–8

1 ▲ Remove the grapes from their stems. Wash them well, and pat dry with paper towels. Place in a bowl and sprinkle with the sugar. Set aside until they are needed.

2 ▲ Knead the dough lightly. Divide it into two halves. Roll out or press one half into a circle about ½ inch thick. Place on a lightly oiled flat cookie sheet. Sprinkle with half of the sugared grapes.

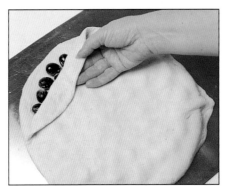

3 ▲ Roll out or press the second half of the dough into a circle the same size as the first. Place it on top of the first.

4 ▲ Crimp the edges together. Sprinkle the top with the remaining grapes. Cover the dough with a dish towel and leave in a warm place to rise for 30 minutes. Preheat the oven to 375°F. Sprinkle the bread with the oil, and bake for 50–60 minutes. Allow to cool before cutting into wedges.

Focaccia

Focaccia

Focaccia is an antique form of flat bread which is oiled before baking. It is usually made in a large cookie sheet, and sold in bakeries cut into squares.

Ingredients
1 recipe Basic Pizza Dough, risen once
3 tbsp olive oil
coarse sea salt
serves 6–8 as a side dish

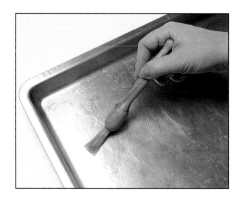

1 ▲ After punching the dough down, knead it for 3–4 minutes. Brush a large shallow baking pan with 1 tbsp of oil.

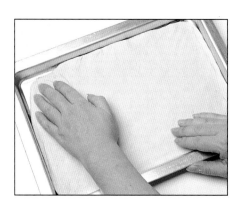

2 ▲ Place the dough in the pan, and use your fingers to press it into an even layer 1 in thick. Cover the dough with a cloth, and leave to rise in a warm place for 30 minutes. Preheat the oven to 400°F.

~ COOK'S TIP ~

To freeze, allow to cool to room temperature after baking. Wrap in foil and freeze. Thaw and place in a warm oven before serving.

3 ▲ Just before baking, use your fingers to press rows of light indentations into the surface of the focaccia dough.

4 ▲ Brush with the remaining oil, and sprinkle lightly with coarse salt. Bake for about 25 minutes, or until just golden. Cut into squares or wedges and serve as an accompaniment to a meal, or alone, warm or at room temperature.

Focaccia with Olives

Focaccia con olive

For this topping, pieces of pitted green olives are pressed onto the dough before baking.

Ingredients

1 recipe Basic Pizza Dough, risen once
3 tbsp olive oil
10–12 large green olives, pitted and cut in half lengthwise
coarse sea salt
serves 6–8 as a side dish

1 After punching the dough down, knead it for 3–4 minutes. Brush a large shallow baking pan with 1 tbsp of the oil. Place the dough in the pan, and use your fingers to press it into an even layer 1 inch thick. Cover the dough with a cloth, and leave to rise in a warm place for 30 minutes. Preheat the oven to 400°F for 30 minutes during this time.

2 ▲ Just before baking, use your fingers to press rows of light indentations into the surface of the focaccia. Brush with the remaining oil.

3 ▲ Dot evenly with the olive pieces, and sprinkle with a little coarse salt. Bake for about 25 minutes, or until just golden. Cut into squares or wedges and serve as an accompaniment to a meal, or alone, warm or at room temperature.

Focaccia with Rosemary

Focaccia con rosmarino

One of the most popular breads. If possible, use fresh rosemary for this recipe.

Ingredients

1 recipe Basic Pizza Dough, risen once
3 tbsp olive oil
2 medium sprigs fresh rosemary, coarse stalks removed
coarse sea salt
serves 6–8 as a side dish

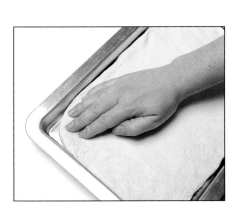

1 ▲ After punching the dough down, knead it for 3–4 minutes. Brush a large shallow baking pan with 1 tbsp of the oil. Place the dough in the pan, and use your fingers to press it into an even layer 1 inch thick.

2 ▲ Scatter with the rosemary leaves. Cover the dough with a cloth, and leave to rise in a warm place for 30 minutes. Preheat the oven to 400°F for 30 minutes during this time.

3 ▲ Just before baking, use your fingers to press rows of light indentations into the surface of the focaccia. Brush with the remaining oil, and sprinkle lightly with coarse salt. Bake for about 25 minutes, or until just golden. Cut into squares or wedges and serve as an accompaniment to a meal, or alone, warm or at room temperature.

Pan-Fried Marinated Poussin

Galletti marinati in padella

These small birds are full of flavor when marinated for several hours before cooking.

Ingredients
2 poussins, about 1 lb each
5–6 leaves fresh mint, torn into pieces
1 leek, sliced into thin rings
1 clove garlic, finely chopped
salt and coarsely ground black pepper
4 tbsp olive oil
2 tbsp fresh lemon juice
¼ cup dry white wine
mint leaves, to garnish
serves 3–4

1 Cut the poussins in half down the backbone, dividing the breast. Flatten the 4 halves with a mallet. Place them in a bowl with the mint, leeks, garlic and pepper. Sprinkle with oil and half the lemon juice, cover, and allow to stand in a cool place for 6 hours.

2 ▲ Heat a large heavy frying pan or skillet. Place the poussins and their marinade in the pan, cover, and cook over moderate heat for about 45 minutes, turning them occasionally. Season with salt during the cooking. Remove to a warm serving platter.

3 ▲ Tilt the pan and spoon off any fat on the surface. Pour in the wine and remaining lemon juice, and cook until the sauce reduces. Strain the sauce, pressing the vegetables to extract all the juices. Place the poussins on individual dishes, and spoon over the sauce. Sprinkle with mint, and serve.

Quail with Grapes

Quaglie con uva

Small birds often feature in Italian recipes. Use the most flavorful white grapes for this dish.

Ingredients
6–8 fresh quail, gutted
salt and freshly ground black pepper
4 tbsp olive oil
¼ cup pancetta or bacon, cut into small
    dice
1 cup dry white wine
1 cup fresh or canned chicken stock,
    warmed
12 oz green grapes
serves 4

1 Wash the quail carefully inside and out with cold water. Pat dry with paper towels. Sprinkle salt and pepper into the cavities.

2 Heat the oil in a heavy sauté pan or flameproof casserole large enough to accommodate all the quail in one layer. Add the pancetta or bacon, and cook over low heat for 5 minutes.

3 ▲ Raise the heat to moderate to high, and place the quail in the pan. Brown them evenly on all sides. Pour in the wine, and cook over moderate heat until it reduces by about half. Turn the quail over. Cover the pan, and cook for about 10–15 minutes. Add the stock, turn the quail again, cover, and cook for 15–20 minutes more, or until the birds are tender. Remove to a warmed serving platter and keep warm while the sauce is being finished.

4 ▲ Meanwhile drop the grapes into a pan of boiling water, and blanch for about 3 minutes. Drain and reserve.

5 Strain the pan juices into a small Pyrex cup. If bacon has been used, allow the fat to separate and rise to the top. Spoon off the fat and discard. Pour the strained gravy into a small saucepan. Add the grapes and warm them gently for 2–3 minutes. Spoon around the quail and serve.

Duck with Chestnut Sauce
Petti di anatra con salsa di castagne

This autumnal dish makes use of the sweet chestnuts that are gathered in Italian woods.

Ingredients
1 sprig fresh rosemary
1 clove garlic, thinly sliced
2 tbsp olive oil
4 duck breasts, boned and fat removed
For the sauce
1 lb chestnuts
1 tsp oil
1½ cups milk
1 small onion, finely chopped
1 carrot, finely chopped
1 small bay leaf
salt and freshly ground black pepper
2 tbsp cream, warmed
serves 4–5

1 ▲ Pull the leaves from the sprig of rosemary. Combine them with the garlic and oil in a shallow bowl. Pat the duck breasts dry with paper towels. Brush the duck breasts with the marinade. Allow to stand for at least 2 hours before cooking.

2 Preheat the oven to 350°F. Cut a cross in the flat side of each chestnut with a sharp knife.

~ COOK'S TIP ~

The chestnut sauce may be prepared in advance and kept in the refrigerator for up to 2 days, or it may be made when chestnuts are in season and frozen. Allow to thaw to room temperature before re-heating.

3 ▲ Place the chestnuts in a baking pan with the oil, and shake the pan until the nuts are coated with the oil. Bake for about 20 minutes, then peel.

4 Place the peeled chestnuts in a heavy saucepan with the milk, onion, carrot and bay leaf. Cook slowly for about 10–15 minutes until the chestnuts are very tender. Season with salt and pepper. Discard the bay leaf. Press the mixture through a strainer.

5 Return the sauce to the saucepan. Heat gently while the duck is cooking. Just before serving, stir in the cream. If the sauce is too thick, add a little more cream. Preheat the broiler, or prepare a barbecue.

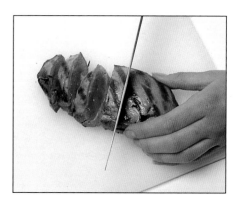

6 ▲ Broil the duck breasts until medium rare, about 6–8 minutes. The meat should be pink when sliced. Slice into rounds and arrange on warm plates. Serve with the heated sauce.

Roast Pheasant with Juniper Berries

Fagiano arrosto

Sage and juniper are often used in Italian cooking to flavor pheasant and other game.

Ingredients

2½–3 lb pheasant with liver, finely chopped (optional)
3 tbsp olive oil
2 sprigs fresh sage
3 shallots, chopped
1 bay leaf
2 lemon quarters, plus 1 tsp juice
2 tbsp juniper berries, lightly crushed
salt and freshly ground black pepper
4 thin slices pancetta or bacon
6 tbsp dry white wine
1 cup fresh or canned chicken stock, heated
2 tbsp butter, at room temperature
2 tbsp flour
2 tbsp brandy
serves 3–4

1 ▲ Wash the pheasant under cool water. Drain well, and pat dry with paper towels. Rub with 1 tbsp of the olive oil. Place the remaining oil, sage leaves, shallots, and bay leaf in a shallow bowl. Add the lemon juice and juniper berries. Place the pheasant and lemon quarters in the bowl with the marinade, and spoon it over the bird. Allow to stand for several hours in a cool place, turning the pheasant occasionally. Remove the lemon.

2 Preheat the oven to 350°F. Place the pheasant in a roasting pan, reserving the marinade. Sprinkle the cavity with salt and pepper, and place the lemon quarters and bay leaf inside.

3 Arrange some of the sage leaves on the breast of the pheasant, and lay the pancetta or bacon over the top. Secure with string.

4 ▲ Spoon the remaining marinade on top of the pheasant, and roast until tender, about 30 minutes per 1 lb. Baste frequently with the pan juices and with the white wine. Transfer the pheasant to a warmed serving platter, discarding the string and pancetta.

5 Tilt the baking pan and skim off any surface fat. Pour in the stock. Stir over moderate heat, scraping up any meat residues from the bottom of the pan. Add the pheasant liver, if using. Bring to a boil and cook for 2–3 minutes. Strain into a saucepan.

6 ▲ Blend the butter to a paste with the flour. Stir into the gravy a little at a time. Boil for 2–3 minutes, stirring to smooth out any lumps. Remove from the heat, stir in the brandy, and serve.

Italian Trifle

Zuppa inglese

Known in Italy as "English Soup" this is a kind of trifle that has little to do with England!

Ingredients

2 cups milk
grated zest of ½ scrubbed lemon
4 egg yolks
⅓ cup superfine sugar
½ cup flour, sifted
1 tbsp rum or brandy
2 tbsp butter
7 oz lady fingers or 11 oz sponge cake,
    sliced into ½ inch slices
⅓ cup kirsch wasser or cherry brandy
⅓ cup Strega liqueur
3 tbsp apricot jam
fresh whipped cream, to garnish
chopped toasted nuts, to garnish
serves 6–8

1 Heat the milk with the lemon zest in a small saucepan. Remove from the heat as soon as small bubbles form on the surface.

2 ▲ Beat the egg yolks with a wire whisk. Gradually incorporate the sugar, and continue beating until pale yellow. Beat in the flour. Stir in the milk very gradually, pouring it in through a strainer to remove the lemon. When all the milk has been added, pour the mixture into a heavy saucepan. Bring to a boil stirring constantly with a whisk. Simmer for 5–6 minutes, stirring constantly. Remove from the heat and stir in the rum or brandy. Beat in the butter. Allow to cool to room temperature, stirring to prevent a skin from forming.

3 ▲ Brush the cookies or cake slices with the kirsch or cherry brandy on one side, and the Strega liqueur on the other. Spread a thin layer of the custard over the bottom of a serving dish. Line the dish with a layer of cookies or cake slices. Cover with some of the custard. Add another layer of cookies which have been brushed with liqueur.

4 ▲ Heat the jam in a small saucepan with 2 tbsp water. When it is hot, pour or brush it evenly over the cookies. Continue with layers of custard and liqueur-brushed cookies until the ingredients have been used up. End with custard. Cover with plastic wrap or foil, and refrigerate for at least 2–3 hours. To serve, decorate the top of the trifle with whipped cream and garnish with chopped nuts.

Chestnut Pudding

Budino di castagne

Sweet chestnuts are found in the mountainous regions of Italy in October and November.

Ingredients

1 lb fresh sweet chestnuts
1¼ cups milk
½ cup sugar
2 eggs, separated, at room temperature
¼ cup unsweetened cocoa powder
½ tsp pure vanilla extract
⅓ cup confectioners' sugar, sifted
butter, for the mold(s)
fresh whipped cream, to garnish
marrons glacés, to garnish
serves 4–5

1 Cut a cross in the side of the chestnuts, and drop them into a pan of boiling water. Cook for 5–6 minutes. Remove with a slotted spoon, and peel while still warm.

2 ▲ Place the peeled chestnuts in a heavy or non-stick saucepan with the milk and half of the sugar. Cook over low heat, stirring occasionally, until soft. Remove from the heat and allow to cool. Press the contents of the pan through a strainer.

3 Preheat the oven to 350°F. Beat the egg yolks with the remaining sugar until the mixture is pale yellow and fluffy. Beat in the cocoa powder and the vanilla.

3 ▲ In a separate bowl, whisk the egg whites with a wire whisk or electric beater until they form soft peaks. Gradually beat in the sifted confectioners' sugar and continue beating until the mixture forms stiff peaks.

4 ▲ Fold the chestnut and egg yolk mixtures together. Fold in the egg whites. Turn the mixture into one large or several individual buttered pudding molds. Place on a cookie sheet, and bake in the oven for 12–20 minutes, depending on the size. Remove from the oven, and allow to cool for 10 minutes before unmolding. Serve garnished with whipped cream and marrons glacés.

Southern Italy

Campania, Apulia, Basilicata, Calabria and Sicily – the five regions that make up Southern Italy – are collectively known as the *Mezzogiorno*, or the land where the sun hangs at midday. It is an area of extreme poverty, so different from the rest of Italy that it might be another country.

Here the countryside is breathtakingly beautiful and unspoiled, and the lack of development in the culture has kept the cuisine of the area closer to its roots than in any other part of Italy. The classic dishes are robust, simple and highly seasoned and the traditional cuisine *cucina rustica*, relies heavily on herbs, peppers, olives, capers and garlic.

Mixed Seafood Salad

Insalata di frutti di mare

All along Italy's coasts versions of this salad appear. Use fresh seafood that is in season, or use a combination of fresh and frozen.

Ingredients

12 oz small squid
1 small onion, cut into quarters
1 bay leaf
7 oz shrimp, in their shells
1½ lb fresh mussels, in their
    shells
1 lb fresh small clams
¾ cup white wine
1 fennel bulb

For the dressing

5 tbsp extra-virgin olive oil
3 tbsp fresh lemon juice
1 clove garlic, finely chopped
salt and freshly ground black pepper

serves 6–8

1 ▲ Working near the sink, clean the squid by first peeling off the thin skin from the body section. Rinse well. Pull the head and tentacles away from the sac section. Some of the intestines will come away with the head. Remove and discard the translucent quill and any remaining insides from the sac. Sever the tentacles from the head. Discard the head and intestines. Remove the small hard beak from the base of the tentacles. Rinse the sac and tentacles well under cold running water. Drain.

2 Bring a large pan of water to a boil. Add the onion and bay leaf. Drop in the squid and cook for about 10 minutes, or until tender. Remove with a slotted spoon, and allow to cool before slicing into rings ½ in wide. Cut each tentacle section into 2 pieces. Set aside.

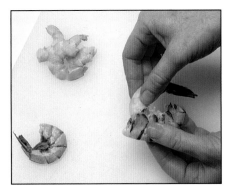

3 ▲ Drop the shrimp into the same boiling water, and cook until they turn pink, about 2 minutes. Remove with a slotted spoon. Peel and devein. (The cooking liquid may be strained and kept for soup.)

4 ▲ Cut off the "beards" from the mussels. Scrub and rinse the mussels and clams well in several changes of cold water. Place in a large saucepan with the wine. Cover, and steam until all the shells have opened. (Discard any that do not open.) Lift the clams and mussels out.

5 ▲ Remove all the clams from their shells with a small spoon. Place in a large serving bowl. Remove all but 8 of the mussels from their shells, and add them to the clams in the bowl. Leave the remaining mussels in their half shells, and set aside. Cut the green, ferny part of the fennel away from the bulb. Chop finely and set aside. Chop the bulb into bite-size pieces, and add it to the serving bowl with the squid and shrimp.

6 ▲ Make a dressing by combining the oil, lemon juice, garlic and chopped fennel green in a small bowl. Add salt and pepper to taste. Pour over the salad, and toss well. Decorate with the remaining mussels in the half shell. This salad may be served at room temperature or slightly chilled.

Prosciutto with Figs

Prosciutto crudo con fichi

The hams cured in the region of Parma are held to be the finest in Italy. Prosciutto makes an excellent starter sliced paper-thin and served with fresh figs or melon.

Ingredients
8 ripe green or black figs
12 paper-thin slices prosciutto crudo
crusty bread, to serve
unsalted butter, to serve
serves 4

2 ▲ Wipe the figs with a damp cloth. Cut them almost into quarters but do not cut all the way through the base. If the skins are tender, they may be eaten along with the inner fruit. If you prefer, you may peel each quarter carefully by pulling the peel gently away from the pulp.

3 ▲ Arrange the figs on top of the prosciutto. Serve with bread and unsalted butter.

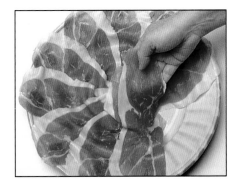

1 ▲ Arrange the slices of prosciutto on a serving plate.

Cherry Tomatoes with Pesto

Pomodorini con pesto

These make a colorful and tasty appetizer to go with drinks, or as part of a buffet. Make the pesto when fresh basil is plentiful, and freeze it in batches.

Ingredients
1 lb cherry tomatoes (about 36)
For the pesto
1 cup fresh basil
3–4 cloves garlic
4 tbsp pine nuts
1 tsp salt, plus extra to taste
7 tbsp olive oil
3 tbsp freshly grated Parmesan
   cheese
6 tbsp freshly grated pecorino
   cheese
freshly ground black pepper
serves 8–10 as an appetizer

1 Wash the tomatoes. Slice off the top of each tomato, and carefully scoop out the seeds with a melon baller or small spoon.

2 ▲ Place the basil, garlic, pine nuts, salt and olive oil in a blender or food processor and process until smooth. Remove the contents to a bowl with a rubber spatula. If desired, the pesto may be frozen at this point, before the cheeses are added. To use when frozen, allow to thaw, then proceed to step 3.

3 Fold in the grated cheeses (use all Parmesan if pecorino is not available). Season with pepper, and more salt if necessary.

4 ▲ Use a small spoon to fill each tomato with a little pesto. This dish is at its best if chilled for about an hour before serving.

Stuffed Mussels

Cozze gratinate

This tasty appetizer is a speciality of southern Italy. It can be made equally well using large clams. Always use the freshest seafood available.

Ingredients

1½ lb large fresh mussels in their shells
⅓ cup unsalted butter, at room temperature
¼ cup dry breadcrumbs
2 cloves garlic, finely chopped
3 tbsp chopped fresh parsley
¼ cup freshly grated Parmesan cheese
salt and freshly ground black pepper

serves 4

1 ▲ Scrub the mussels well under cold running water, cutting off the "beard" with a small knife. Preheat the oven to 450°F.

2 ▲ Place the mussels with a cupful of water in a large saucepan over moderate heat. As soon as they open, lift them out one by one. Remove and discard the empty half shells, leaving the mussels in the other half. (Discard any mussels that do not open.)

3 ▲ Combine all the remaining ingredients in a small bowl. Blend well. Place in a small saucepan and heat gently until the stuffing mixture begins to soften.

4 ▲ Arrange the mussel halves on a flat cookie sheet. Spoon a small amount of the stuffing over each mussel. Bake for about 7 minutes, or until lightly browned. Serve hot or at room temperature.

Stuffed Artichokes

Carciofi ripieni

Artichokes grow almost wild in southern Italy and they are cooked in many different ways. In this recipe the artichokes are stuffed and baked whole.

Ingredients

1 lemon

6 large globe artichokes

For the stuffing

2 slices white bread, crusts removed (about 2 oz)

3 anchovy fillets, finely chopped

2 cloves garlic, finely chopped

2 tbsp capers, rinsed and finely chopped

3 tbsp finely chopped fresh parsley

4 tbsp plain dry breadcrumbs

4 tbsp olive oil

salt and freshly ground black pepper

For baking

1 clove garlic, cut into 3 or 4 pieces

1 sprig fresh parsley

3 tbsp olive oil

serves 6

1 Prepare the stuffing. Soak the white bread in a little water for 5 minutes. Squeeze dry. Place in a bowl with the other stuffing ingredients and mix.

2 ▲ Squeeze the lemon, and put the juice and the squeezed halves in a large bowl of cold water. Wash the artichokes and prepare them one at a time. Cut off only the tip from the stem. Peel the stem with a small knife, pulling upwards towards the leaves. Pull off the small leaves around the stem, and continue snapping off the upper part of the dark outer leaves until you reach the taller inner leaves. Cut off the topmost part of these leaves with a sharp knife.

3 ▲ Open the artichoke slightly by spreading the leaves apart to get at the inner bristly "choke". Cut around it with the knife, and scrape it out with a small spoon. This forms a cavity inside the artichoke leaves. As soon as each artichoke has been prepared, place it in the bowl of acidulated water. This will prevent it from darkening. Preheat the oven to 375°F.

4 ▲ Place the garlic and the parsley leaves in a baking dish large enough to hold the artichokes upright in one layer. Pour in cold water to a depth of ½ inch. Remove the artichokes from the bowl, drain quickly, and fill the cavities with the stuffing. Place the artichokes upside down in the dish. Pour a little oil over each. Cover the dish tightly with foil. Bake for about 1 hour, or until tender.

Eggplant Parmesan

Parmigiana di melanzane

This famous dish is a speciality of Italy's southern regions.

Ingredients
2 lb eggplants
flour, for coating
oil, for frying
⅓ cup freshly grated Parmesan cheese
2 cups mozzarella cheese, sliced very
    thinly
salt and freshly ground black pepper
For the tomato sauce
4 tbsp olive oil
1 medium onion, very finely chopped
1 clove garlic, finely chopped
1 lb tomatoes, fresh or canned, chopped,
    with their juice
salt and freshly ground black pepper
a few leaves fresh basil or sprigs parsley
serves 4–6

1 Wash the eggplants. Cut into rounds about ½ inch wide, sprinkle with salt, and leave to drain for about 1 hour.

2 ▲ Meanwhile make the tomato sauce. Heat the oil in a medium saucepan. Add the onion, and cook over moderate heat until it is translucent, 5–8 minutes. Stir in the garlic and the tomatoes (add 3 tbsp of water if you are using fresh tomatoes). Season with salt and pepper. Add the basil or parsley. Cook for 20–30 minutes. Purée in a food mill or a food processor.

3 Pat the eggplant slices dry with paper towels. Coat lightly in flour. Heat a little oil in a large frying pan (preferably non-stick). Add one layer of eggplant, and cook over low to moderate heat with the pan covered until soft. Turn, and cook on the other side. Remove from the pan, and repeat with the remaining slices.

4 Preheat the oven to 350°F. Grease a wide shallow baking dish or pan. Spread a little tomato sauce in the bottom. Cover with a layer of eggplant. Sprinkle with a few teaspoons of Parmesan, season with salt and pepper, and cover with a layer of mozzarella. Spoon on some tomato sauce. Repeat until all the ingredients are used up, ending with a covering of tomato sauce and a sprinkling of Parmesan. Sprinkle with a little olive oil, and bake for about 45 minutes.

Sweet and Sour Eggplant

Caponata

This delicious Sicilian dish combines eggplant and celery in a piquant sauce.

Ingredients
1½ lb eggplants
2 tbsp olive oil
1 medium onion, finely sliced
1 clove garlic, finely chopped
1 × 8 oz can plum tomatoes, peeled and
    finely chopped
½ cup white wine vinegar
2 tbsp sugar
salt and freshly ground black pepper
tender central stalks of a head of celery
    (about 6 oz)
2 tbsp capers, rinsed
½ cup green olives, pitted
oil, for deep-frying
2 tbsp chopped fresh parsley
serves 4

1 Wash the eggplants and cut into small cubes. Sprinkle with salt, and leave to drain in a colander for 1 hour.

2 ▲ Heat the oil in a large saucepan. Stir in the onion, and cook until soft. Stir in the garlic and tomatoes, and fry over moderate heat for 10 minutes. Stir in the vinegar, sugar and pepper. Simmer until the sauce reduces, 10 more. Blanch the celery stalks in boiling water until tender. Drain, and chop into 1 in pieces. Add to the sauce with the capers and olives.

3 ▲ Pat the eggplant cubes dry with paper towels. Heat the oil to 360°F, and deep-fry the eggplant in batches until golden. Drain on paper towels.

4 Add the eggplant to the sauce. Stir gently and season. Stir in the parsley. Allow to stand for 30 minutes. Serve at room temperature.

Carrots with Marsala

Carote al marsala

The sweet flavor of marsala goes surprisingly well with carrots in this Sicilian dish.

Ingredients
4 tbsp butter
1 lb carrots, thinly sliced
1 tsp sugar
½ tsp salt
¼ cup marsala
serves 4

1 Melt the butter in a medium saucepan, and add the carrots. Stir well to coat with the butter. Add the sugar and salt, and mix well.

2 ▲ Stir in the marsala, and simmer for 4–5 minutes.

3 ▲ Pour in enough water to barely cover the carrots. Cover the pan, and cook over low to moderate heat until the carrots are tender. Remove the cover, and cook until the liquids reduce almost completely. Serve hot.

Broccoli with Oil and Garlic

Broccoletti saltati con aglio

This is a very simple way of transforming steamed or blanched broccoli into a succulent Mediterranean dish. Peeling the broccoli stalks is easy, and allows for even cooking.

Ingredients
2 lb fresh broccoli
6 tbsp olive oil
2–3 cloves garlic, finely chopped
salt and freshly ground black pepper
serves 6

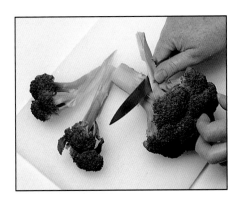

1 ▲ Wash the broccoli. Cut off any woody parts at the base of the stems. Use a small sharp knife to peel the broccoli stems. Cut any very long or wide stalks in half.

2 ▲ Boil water in the bottom of a saucepan equipped with a steamer, or bring a large pan of water to a boil. If steaming the broccoli, put it in the steamer and cover tightly. Cook for 8–12 minutes or until the stems are just tender when pierced with the point of a knife. Remove from the heat. If blanching, drop the broccoli into the pan of boiling water and blanch until just tender, 5–6 minutes. Drain.

3 ▲ In a frying pan large enough to hold all the broccoli pieces, gently heat the oil with the garlic. When the garlic is light golden (do not let it brown or it will be bitter) add the broccoli, and cook over moderate heat for 3–4 minutes, turning carefully to coat it with the hot oil. Season with salt and pepper. Serve hot or cold.

Potatoes Baked with Tomatoes

Patate e pomodori al forno

This simple, hearty dish from the south of Italy is best when tomatoes are in season, but can also be made with canned plum tomatoes.

Ingredients

2 large red or yellow onions, thinly sliced
2 lb potatoes, peeled and thinly sliced
1 lb tomatoes, fresh or canned, sliced, with their juice
6 tbsp olive oil
1 cup freshly grated Parmesan or Romano
salt and freshly ground black pepper
a few leaves fresh basil
¼ cup water

serves 6

1 Preheat the oven to 350°F. Brush a large baking dish generously with oil.

2 ▲ Arrange a layer of onions in the dish, followed by layers of potatoes and tomatoes. Pour on a little of the oil, and sprinkle with the cheese. Season with salt and pepper.

layer of potatoes and tomatoes. Tear the basil leaves into pieces, and add them here and there among the vegetables. Sprinkle the top with cheese, and a little oil.

5 ▲ If the top begins to brown too much, place a sheet of foil or a flat cookie sheet on top of the dish. Serve hot.

3 ▲ Repeat until the vegetables are used up, ending with an overlapping

4 ▲ Pour on the water. Bake for 1 hour, or until tender.

Tomatoes with Pasta Stuffing

Pomodori ripieni di pasta

Tomatoes are one of Italy's staple foods, appearing in more than three-quarters of all Italian savory dishes. They can be baked with various stuffings. This one comes from the south.

Ingredients

8 large tomatoes, firm and ripe
1¼ cups small soup pasta
8 black olives, pitted and finely chopped
3 tbsp finely chopped mixed fresh herbs, such as chives, parsley, basil and thyme
4 tbsp grated Parmesan cheese
4 tbsp olive oil
salt and freshly ground black pepper
serves 4

1 ▲ Wash the tomatoes. Slice off the tops, and scoop out the pulp with a small spoon. Chop the pulp and turn the tomatoes upside down on a rack to drain.

2 ▲ Place the pulp in a strainer, and allow the juices to drain off. Meanwhile, boil the pasta in a pan of boiling salted water. Drain it 2 minutes before the recommended cooking time elapses.

3 ▲ Preheat the oven to 375°F. Combine the pasta with the remaining ingredients in a bowl. Stir in the drained tomato pulp. Season with salt and pepper.

4 ▲ Stuff the tomatoes, and replace the tops. Arange them in one layer in a well-oiled baking dish. Bake for 15–20 minutes. Peel off the skins, if desired. Serve hot or at room temperature.

Fusilli with Peppers and Onions

Fusilli con peperoni

Peppers are characteristic of southern Italy. When broiled and peeled they have a delicious smoky flavor, and are easier to digest.

Ingredients

1 lb red and yellow peppers
    (about 2 large ones)
6 tbsp olive oil
1 large red onion, thinly sliced
2 cloves garlic, minced
1 lb fusilli or other short pasta
salt and freshly ground black pepper
3 tbsp finely chopped fresh parsley
freshly grated Parmesan cheese, to serve
serves 4

1 ▲ Place the peppers under a hot broiler and turn occasionally until they are black and blistered on all sides. Remove from the heat, place in a paper bag and leave for 5 minutes.

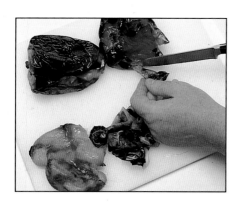

2 ▲ Peel the peppers. Cut them into quarters, remove the stems and seeds, and slice into thin strips. Bring a large pan of water to a boil.

3 ▲ Heat the oil in a large frying pan. Add the onion, and cook over moderate heat until it is translucent, 5–8 minutes. Stir in the garlic, and cook for 2 minutes more.

4 ▲ Add salt and the pasta to the boiling water, and cook until the pasta is just *al dente*.

~ COOK'S TIP ~

Peppers belong to the *capsicum annum* family. They were brought to Europe by Columbus who discovered them in Haiti. The large red, yellow and orange peppers are usually sweeter than the green varieties, and have a fuller flavor.

5 ▲ Meanwhile, add the peppers to the onions, and mix together gently. Stir in about 3 tbsp of the pasta cooking water. Season with salt and pepper. Stir in the parsley.

6 ▲ Drain the pasta. Tip it into the frying pan with the vegetables, and cook over moderate heat for 1–2 minutes, stirring constantly to mix the pasta into the sauce. Serve with the Parmesan passed separately.

Orecchiette with Broccoli
Pasta e broccoli

Puglia, in southern Italy, specializes in imaginative pasta and vegetable combinations. Using the broccoli cooking water for boiling the pasta gives it more of the vegetable's flavor.

Ingredients
1¾ lb broccoli
1 lb orecchiette or penne
6 tbsp olive oil
3 cloves garlic, finely chopped
6 anchovy fillets in oil
salt and freshly ground black pepper
serves 6

1 Peel the stems of the broccoli, starting from the base and pulling up towards the florets with a knife. Discard the woody parts of the stem. Cut florets and stems into 2 in pieces.

2 ▲ Bring a large pan of water to a boil. Drop in the broccoli, and boil until barely tender, about 5–8 minutes. Remove the broccoli pieces from the pan to a serving bowl. Do not discard the cooking water.

3 ▲ Add salt to the broccoli cooking water. Bring it back to a boil. Drop in the pasta, stir well, and cook until it is *al dente*.

4 ▲ While the pasta is boiling, heat the oil in a small frying pan. Add the garlic and, after 2–3 minutes, the anchovy fillets. Using a fork, mash the anchovies and garlic to a paste. Cook for 3–4 minutes more.

5 ▲ Before draining the pasta, ladle 1–2 cupfuls of the cooking water over the broccoli. Add the drained pasta and the hot anchovy and oil mixture. Mix well, and season with salt and pepper if necessary. Serve at once.

Spaghetti with Olives and Capers   *Spaghetti alla puttanesca*

This spicy sauce originated in the Naples area, where it was named for the local women of easy virtue. It can be quickly assembled using a few kitchen cupboard staples.

Ingredients

4 tbsp olive oil
2 cloves garlic, finely chopped
small piece of dried chili, crumbled
1 × 2 oz can of anchovy fillets, chopped
12 oz tomatoes, fresh or canned,
　chopped
⅔ cup pitted black olives
2 tbsp capers, rinsed
1 tbsp tomato paste
1 lb spaghetti
2 tbsp chopped fresh parsley, to serve

serves 4

1 ▲ Bring a large pan of water to a boil. Heat the oil in a large frying pan. Add the garlic and the dried chili, and cook for 2–3 minutes until the garlic is just golden.

2 ▲ Add the anchovies, and mash them into the garlic with a fork.

3 ▲ Add the tomatoes, olives, capers and tomato paste. Stir well and cook over moderate heat.

4 Add salt to the boiling water, and put in the spaghetti. Stir, and cook until the pasta is just *al dente*. Drain.

5 ▲ Turn the spaghetti into the sauce. Raise the heat, and cook for 1–2 minutes, turning the pasta constantly. Sprinkle with parsley if desired and serve. Traditionally, no cheese is served with this sauce.

Spaghetti with Mussels

Spaghetti con cozze

Mussels are popular in all the coastal regions of Italy, and are delicious with pasta. This simple dish is greatly improved by using the freshest mussels available.

Ingredients

2 lb fresh mussels, in their shells
5 tbsp olive oil
3 cloves garlic, finely chopped
4 tbsp finely chopped fresh parsley
4 tbsp white wine
1 lb spaghetti
salt and freshly ground black pepper

serves 4

1 ▲ Scrub the mussels well under cold running water, cutting off the "beard" with a small sharp knife.

2 ▲ Bring a large pan of water to a boil for the pasta. Place the mussels with a cupful of water in another large saucepan over moderate heat. As soon as they open, lift them out one by one.

3 ▲ When all the mussels have opened (discard any that do not), strain the liquid in the saucepan through a layer of paper towels and reserve until needed.

4 ▲ Heat the oil in a large frying pan. Add the garlic and parsley, and cook for 2–3 minutes. Add the mussels, their strained juices and the wine. Cook over moderate heat. Meanwhile add salt to the boiling water, and drop in the pasta.

5 ▲ Add a generous amount of freshly ground black pepper to the sauce. Taste for seasoning, adding salt as necessary.

6 ▲ Drain the pasta when it is *al dente*. Tip it into the frying pan with the sauce, and stir well over moderate heat for 1–2 minutes more. Serve at once, without cheese.

~ COOK'S TIP ~

Mussels should be firmly closed when fresh. If a mussel is slightly open, pinch it closed. If it remains closed on its own, it is alive. If it remains open, discard it. Fresh mussels should be consumed as soon as possible after being purchased. They may be kept in a bowl of cold water in the refrigerator.

Pasta with Fresh Sardine Sauce
Pasta con sarde

In this classic Sicilian dish, fresh sardines are combined with raisins and pine nuts.

Ingredients

3 tbsp sultanas
1 lb fresh sardines
6 tbsp breadcrumbs
1 small fennel bulb
6 tbsp olive oil
1 medium onion, very thinly sliced
3 tbsp pine nuts
½ tsp fennel seeds
salt and freshly ground black pepper
1 lb long hollow pasta such as percatelli,
    ziti, or bucatini

serves 4

1 Soak the sultanas in warm water for
15 minutes. Drain and pat dry.

2 ▲ Clean the sardines. Open each
one out flat and remove the back bone
and head. Wash well and shake dry.
Sprinkle with breadcrumbs.

3 ▲ Coarsely chop the top fronds of
fennel and reserve. Pull off a few outer
leaves and wash. Fill a large pan with
enough water to cook the pasta. Add
the fennel leaves and bring to a boil.

4 ▲ Heat the oil in a large frying pan
and sauté the onion lightly until soft.
Remove to a side dish. Add the
sardines, a few at a time, and cook over
moderate heat until golden on both
sides, turning them once carefully.
When all the sardines have been
cooked, gently return them to the pan.
Add the onion, and the sultanas, pine
nuts and fennel seeds. Season with salt
and pepper.

5 ▲ Take about 4 tbsp of the boiling
water for the pasta, and add it to the
sauce. Add salt to the boiling water,
and drop in the pasta. Cook until it is
al dente. Drain, and remove the fennel
leaves. Dress the pasta with the sauce.
Divide between individual serving
plates, arranging several sardines on
each. Sprinkle with the reserved
chopped fennel tops before serving.

Fried Mozzarella

Mozzarella fritta

These cheese slices make a good informal lunch. They originate from the Neapolitan area, where much mozzarella is produced. They must be made just before serving.

Ingredients

1¾ cups mozzarella cheese
oil, for deep-frying
2 eggs
flour seasoned with salt and freshly
    ground black pepper, for coating
plain dry breadcrumbs, for coating
serves 2–3

3 ▲ Press the cheese slices into the flour, coating them evenly with a thin layer of flour. Shake off any excess. Dip them into the egg, then into the breadcrumbs. Dip them once more into the egg, and then again into the breadcrumbs.

4 ▲ Fry immediately in the hot oil until golden brown. (You may have to do this in two batches but do not let the breaded cheese wait for too long or the breadcrumb coating will separate from the cheese while it is being fried.) Drain quickly on paper towels, and serve hot.

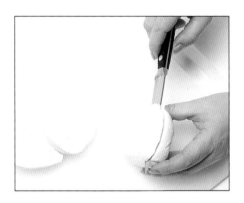

1 ▲ Cut the mozzarella into slices about ½ inch thick. Gently pat off any excess moisture with a paper towel.

2 ▲ Heat the oil until a small piece of bread sizzles as soon as it is dropped in (about 360°F). While the oil is heating beat the eggs in a shallow bowl. Spread some flour on one plate, and some breadcrumbs on another.

Cheese and Tomato Pizza

Pizza alla Margherita

The Margherita is named after the nineteenth-century Queen of Italy, and is one of the most popular of all pizzas.

Ingredients

1 lb peeled plum tomatoes, fresh or canned, weighed whole, without extra juice
1 recipe Basic Pizza Dough, rolled out
1¾ cups mozzarella cheese, cut into small dice
10–12 leaves fresh basil, torn into pieces
4 tbsp freshly grated Parmesan cheese (optional)
salt and freshly ground black pepper
3 tbsp olive oil

serves 4

1 Preheat the oven to 475°F for at least 20 minutes before baking. Strain the tomatoes through the medium holes of a food mill placed over a bowl, scraping in all the pulp.

2 ▲ Spread the puréed tomatoes onto the prepared pizza dough, leaving the rim uncovered.

3 ▲ Sprinkle evenly with the mozzarella. Dot with basil. Sprinkle with Parmesan if using, salt and pepper and olive oil. Immediately place the pizzas in the oven. Bake for about 15–20 minutes, or until the crust is golden brown and the cheeses melted and are bubbling.

Pizza with Mozzarella and Anchovies

Pizza alla napoletana

If you ask for a pizza in the Neapolitan manner anywhere in Italy other than in Naples, you will be given this pizza with anchovies.

Ingredients

1 lb peeled plum tomatoes, fresh or canned, weighed whole, without extra juice
1 recipe Basic Pizza Dough, rolled out
3 tbsp anchovy fillets in oil, drained and cut into pieces
1¾ cups mozzarella cheese, cut into small dice
1 tsp oregano leaves, fresh or dried
salt and freshly ground black pepper
3 tbsp olive oil

serves 4

1 Preheat the oven to 475°F for at least 20 minutes before baking. Strain the tomatoes through the medium holes of a food mill placed over a bowl, scraping in all the pulp.

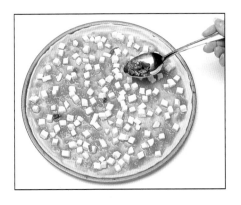

2 ▲ Spread the puréed tomatoes on the pizza dough, leaving the rim uncovered. Dot with the anchovy pieces and the mozzarella.

3 ▲ Sprinkle with oregano, salt and pepper, and olive oil. Immediately place the pizza in the oven. Bake for about 15–20 minutes, or until the crust is golden brown and the cheese is bubbling.

Pizza with Seafood

Pizza con frutti di mare

Any combination of shellfish or other seafood can be used as a pizza topping.

Ingredients

1lb peeled plum tomatoes, fresh or
    canned, weighed whole, without extra
    juice
6 oz small squid
8 oz fresh mussels
1 recipe Basic Pizza Dough, rolled out
6 oz shrimp, raw or cooked, peeled and
    deveined
2 cloves garlic, finely chopped
3 tbsp chopped fresh parsley
salt and freshly ground black pepper
3 tbsp olive oil

serves 4

1 ▲ Preheat the oven to 475°F for at least 20 minutes before baking the pizza. Strain the tomatoes through the medium holes of a food mill placed over a bowl, scraping in all the pulp.

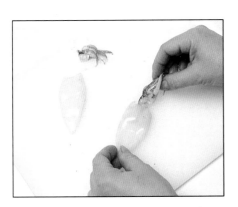

2 ▲ Working near the sink, clean the squid by first peeling off the thin skin from the body section. Rinse well. Pull the head and tentacles away from the sac section. Some of the intestines will come away with the head.

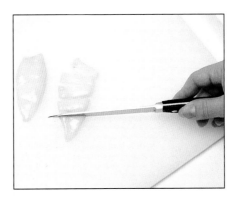

3 ▲ Remove and discard the translucent quill and any remaining insides from the sac. Sever the tentacles from the head. Discard the head and intestines. Remove the small hard beak from the base of the tentacles. Rinse the sac and tentacles under running water. Drain. Slice the sacs into rings ¼ in thick.

4 ▲ Scrape any barnacles off the mussels, and scrub well with a stiff brush. Rinse in several changes of cold water. Place the mussels in a saucepan and heat until they open. Lift them out with a slotted spoon, and remove to a side dish. (Discard any that do not open.) Break off the empty half shells, and discard.

5 ▲ Spread some of the puréed tomatoes on the prepared pizza dough, leaving the rim uncovered. Dot evenly with the shrimp and squid rings and tentacles. Sprinkle with the garlic, parsley, salt and pepper, and olive oil. Immediately place the pizza in the oven. Bake for about 8 minutes.

6 ▲ Remove from the oven, and add the mussels in the half shells. Return to the oven and bake for 7–10 minutes more, or until the crust is golden.

~ VARIATION ~

Fresh clams may be added: scrub them well under cold running water. Place in a saucepan and heat until the shells open. Lift them out and remove to a side dish. Discard any that do not open. Break off the empty half shells, and discard. Add to the pizza after 8 minutes of baking.

Pizza with Herbs

Pizza in bianco con erbe aromatiche

This simple topping of mixed fresh herbs, olive oil and salt make a delicious hot pizza which can also be eaten as a bread. In Italy it is often served in a pizzeria and eaten as an appetizer.

Ingredients

1 recipe Basic Pizza Dough, rolled out
4 tbsp chopped mixed fresh herbs, such as thyme, rosemary, basil, parsley or sage
salt, to taste
6 tbsp extra-virgin olive oil
serves 4

1 ▲ Preheat the oven to 475°F for at least 20 minutes before baking the pizza. Sprinkle the prepared dough with the herbs, and salt.

2 ▲ Sprinkle with olive oil. Immediately place the pizza in the oven. Bake for about 20 minutes, or until the crust is golden brown.

Sicilian Closed Pizza

Sfinciuni

These can be stuffed with any pizza topping.

Ingredients

1 recipe Basic Pizza Dough, risen once
2 tbsp coarse cornmeal
3 hard-boiled eggs, peeled and sliced
¼ cup anchovy fillets, drained and chopped
12 olives, pitted
8 leaves fresh basil, torn into pieces
6 medium tomatoes, peeled, seeded and diced
2 cloves garlic, finely chopped
freshly ground black pepper
1½ cups grated caciocavallo or pecorino cheese
olive oil, for brushing
serves 4–6

1 Preheat the oven to 450°F. Punch the dough and knead lightly for 3–4 minutes. Divide the dough into two pieces, one slightly larger than the other. Lightly oil a round pizza pan 15 inches in diameter. Sprinkle with the cornmeal. Roll or press the larger piece of dough into a round slightly bigger than the pan.

2 ▲ Transfer to the pan, bringing the dough up the sides of the pan to the rim. Fill the pie by placing the sliced eggs in the bottom in a layer, leaving the edges of the dough uncovered. Dot with the anchovies, olives and basil.

3 Spread the diced tomatoes over the other ingredients. Sprinkle with garlic and pepper. Top with the grated cheese.

4 ▲ Roll or press the other piece of dough into a circle the same size as the pan. Place it over the filling. Roll the edge of the bottom dough over it, and crimp together to make a border.

5 Brush the top and edges of the pie with olive oil. Bake for 30–40 minutes, or until the top is golden brown. Allow to stand for 5–8 minutes before slicing into wedges.

Calzone

Calzone

A calzone is a pizza folded over to enclose its filling. It can be made large or small, and stuffed with any of the flat pizza fillings. Calzone can be eaten hot or cold.

Ingredients

1 recipe Basic Pizza Dough, risen once
1½ cups ricotta cheese
¾ cup ham, cut into small dice
6 medium tomatoes, peeled, seeded and
  diced
8 leaves fresh basil, torn into pieces
1 cup mozzarella cheese, cut into small
  dice
4 tbsp freshly grated Parmesan or
  Romano cheese
salt and freshly ground black pepper
olive oil, for brushing

serves 4

3 ▲ Combine all the filling ingredients in a bowl, and mix well. Season with salt and pepper.

5 ▲ Fold the other half of the circle over. Crimp the edges of the dough together with your fingers to seal.

1 ▲ Preheat the oven to 475°F for at least 20 minutes before baking the calzone. Punch the dough down and knead it lightly. Divide the dough into 4 balls.

4 ▲ Divide the filling between the 4 circles of dough, placing it on half of each circle and allowing a border of 1 in all around.

6 ▲ Place the calzone on lightly oiled cookie sheets. Brush the tops lightly with olive oil. Bake in the preheated oven for about 15–20 minutes, or until the tops are golden brown and the dough is puffed.

2 ▲ Roll each ball out into a flat circle about ¼ inch thick.

~ COOK'S TIP ~

The calzone is a speciality of Naples. Calzone means "trouser leg" in Italian. This pizza was so named because it resembled a leg of the baggy trousers worn by Neapolitan men in the 18th and 19th centuries. Calzone are now usually round but were originally made from rectangular pieces of dough folded over a long central filling.

Pizzaiola Steak

Bistecchine alla pizzaiola

This dish comes from Naples, where tomato sauces are used from pizza to meat.

Ingredients
1 lb beef steaks, preferably rump or
    chuck, thinly sliced
3 tbsp flour, for dredging
3 tbsp olive oil
3 cloves garlic, peeled and crushed
1 × 14 oz can plum tomatoes, with their
    juice, passed through a food mill
2 tbsp chopped basil or parsley
salt and freshly ground black pepper
serves 4

1 Trim any excess fat from the steaks, and notch the edges slightly with a sharp knife to prevent them from curling during cooking. Pat the steaks dry with paper towels, and dredge lightly in the flour.

2 ▲ In a large heavy frying pan or skillet, heat 2 tbsp of the oil with the garlic cloves. As soon as they are golden, raise the heat, push them to the side of the pan, and add the steaks. Brown quickly on both sides. Remove the meat to a dish.

3 ▲ Add the tomatoes, the remaining oil, and the herbs to the pan. Season with salt and pepper. Cook over moderate heat for about 15 minutes. Discard the garlic cloves. Return the steaks to the pan, stir to cover them with the sauce, and cook for 4–5 minutes more. Serve.

Herbed Burgers

Polpette

Dress up ground beef with fresh herbs and a tasty tomato sauce.

Ingredients
1½ lb lean ground beef
1 clove garlic, finely chopped
1 scallion, very finely chopped
3 tbsp chopped fresh basil
2 tbsp finely chopped parsley
salt and freshly ground black pepper
3 tbsp butter
For the tomato sauce
3 tbsp olive oil
1 medium onion, finely chopped
11 oz tomatoes, chopped
a few leaves fresh basil
3–4 tbsp water
1 tsp sugar
1 tbsp white wine vinegar
salt and freshly ground black pepper
serves 4

2 Add the water, sugar and vinegar, and cook for 2–3 minutes more. Season with salt and pepper. Remove from the heat, allow to cool slightly, and pass the sauce through a food mill or strainer. Check the seasoning.

1 To make the tomato sauce, heat the oil and gently sauté the onion until translucent. Add the tomatoes and cook for 2–3 minutes. Add the basil, cover the pan, and cook for 7–8 minutes over moderate heat.

3 ▲ Combine the meat with the garlic, scallions and herbs in a mixing bowl. Season with salt and pepper. Form into 4 burgers, patting the meat as lightly as possible.

3 ▲ Heat the butter in a frying pan. When the foam subsides add the burgers, and cook over moderate heat until brown on the underside. Turn the burgers over, and continue cooking until done. Remove to a warmed plate.

4 Tilt the frying pan, and spoon off any surface fat. Pour in the sauce, raise the heat and bring to a boil, scraping up the meat residue from the bottom of the pan. Serve with the burgers.

Roast Lamb with Herbs

Arrosto d'agnello con erbe e aglio

This dish originates from southern Italy, where lamb is simply roasted with garlic and herbs.

Ingredients

3 lb leg of lamb
3–4 tbsp olive oil
4 cloves garlic, peeled and cut in half
2 sprigs fresh sage, or pinch of dried sage leaves
2 sprigs fresh rosemary, or 1 tsp dried rosemary leaves
2 bay leaves
2 sprigs fresh thyme, or ½ tsp dried thyme leaves
salt and freshly ground black pepper
¾ cup dry white wine
serves 4–6

1 Cut any excess fat from the lamb. Rub with olive oil. Using a sharp knife, make small cuts just under the skin all around the meat. Insert the garlic pieces in some of the cuts, and a few of the fresh herbs in the others. (If using dried herbs, sprinkle them over the surface of the meat.)

2 Rub the remaining fresh herbs all over the lamb, and allow it to stand in a cool place for at least 2 hours before cooking. Preheat the oven to 375°F.

3 ▲ Place the lamb in a baking pan, surrounded by the herbs. Pour on 2 tbsp of the oil. Season. Place in the oven and roast for 35 minutes, basting occasionally.

4 ▲ Pour the wine over the lamb. Roast for 15 minutes more, or until the meat is cooked. Remove the lamb to a heated serving dish. Tilt the pan, spooning off any fat on the surface. Strain the pan juices into a gravy boat. Slice the meat, and serve with the sauce passed separately.

Lamb Stewed with Tomatoes and Garlic

Spezzatino d'agnello

This rustic stew comes from the plateau of Puglia, where sheep graze alongside vineyards.

Ingredients

2 large cloves garlic
1 sprig fresh rosemary (or 3 tbsp chopped fresh parsley if fresh rosemary is not available)
6 tbsp olive oil
2½ lb stewing lamb, trimmed of fat and gristle and cut into chunks
flour seasoned with freshly ground black pepper, for dredging
¾ cup dry white wine
2 tsp salt
1 lb fresh tomatoes, chopped, or 1 × 14 oz can tomatoes, chopped
½ cup beef stock, heated
serves 5–6

1 Preheat the oven to 350°F. Chop the garlic with the parsley, if using. Heat 4 tbsp of the oil in a wide casserole.

2 Add the garlic and rosemary or parsley and cook over moderate heat, until the garlic is golden.

3 ▲ Dredge the lamb in the flour. Add the lamb chunks to the pan in one layer, turning to brown them evenly. When brown, remove them to a side plate. Add a little more oil, and brown the remaining lamb.

4 ▲ When all the lamb has been browned, return it to the casserole with the wine. Raise the heat and bring to a boil, scraping up any residues from the bottom. Sprinkle with the salt. Stir in the tomatoes and the stock. Stir well. Cover the casserole, and place in the center of the oven. Bake for 1¾–2 hours, or until the meat is tender.

Coffee Granita

Granita di caffè

A granita is a cross between a frozen drink and a flavored ice. The consistency should be slushy, not solid. They can be made at home with the help of a food processor.

Ingredients
2 cups water
½ cup granulated sugar
1 cup very strong espresso coffee, cooled
whipped cream, to garnish (optional)
serves 4–5

1 ▲ Heat the water and sugar together over low heat until the sugar dissolves. Bring to a boil. Remove from the heat and allow to cool.

2 ▲ Combine the coffee with the sugar syrup. Place in a shallow container or freezer tray, and freeze until solid. Plunge the bottom of the frozen container or tray in very hot water for a few seconds. Turn the frozen mixture out, and chop it into large chunks.

3 ▲ Place the mixture in a food processor fitted with metal blades, and process until it forms small crystals. Spoon into serving glasses and top with whipped cream, if desired. If you do not want to serve the granita immediately, pour the processed mixture back into a shallow container or ice tray and freeze until serving time. Allow to thaw for a few minutes before serving, or process again.

Lemon Granita

Granita di limone

Nothing is more refreshing on a hot summer's day than a fresh lemon granita.

Ingredients
2 cups water
½ cup granulated sugar
grated zest of 1 lemon, scrubbed before
    grating
juice of 2 large lemons
serves 4–5

1 Heat the water and sugar together over low heat until the sugar dissolves. Bring to a boil. Remove from the heat, and allow to cool.

2 Combine the lemon zest and juice with the sugar syrup. Place in a shallow container or freezer tray, and freeze until solid.

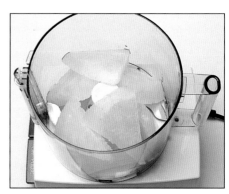

3 ▲ Plunge the bottom of the frozen container or tray in very hot water for a few seconds. Turn the frozen mixture out, and chop it into large chunks.

4 ▲ Place the mixture in a food processor fitted with metal blades, and process until it forms small crystals. Spoon into serving glasses.

Custard Ice Cream

Gelato di crema

Italian ice creams are soft in consistency, and should not be over-sweet.

Ingredients
3½ cups milk
½ tsp grated lemon zest
6 egg yolks
½ cup granulated sugar
makes about 3¾ cups

1 Make the custard. Heat the milk with the lemon zest in a small saucepan. Remove from the heat as soon as small bubbles start to form on the surface. Do not let it boil.

2 Beat the egg yolks with a wire whisk or electric beater. Gradually incorporate the sugar, and continue beating for about 5 minutes until the mixture is pale yellow. Strain the milk. Slowly add it to the egg mixture drop by drop.

3 ▲ When all the milk has been added, pour the mixture into the top of a double boiler, or into a bowl placed over a pan of simmering water. Stir over moderate heat until the water in the pan is boiling, and the custard thickens enough to lightly coat the back of a spoon. Remove from the heat and allow to cool.

4 Freeze in an ice cream maker, following the manufacturer's instructions. The gelato is ready when it is firm but still soft.

5 ▲ If you do not have an ice cream maker, pour the mixture into a metal or plastic freezer container and freeze until set, about 3 hours. Remove from the container and chop roughly into 3 in pieces. Place in the bowl of a food processor and process until smooth. Return to the freezer container, and freeze again until firm. Repeat the freezing-chopping process 2 or 3 times, until a smooth consistency is reached.

Chocolate Ice Cream

Gelato al cioccolato

Use good quality plain or cooking chocolate for the best flavor.

Ingredients
3½ cups milk
4 in piece of vanilla bean
8 oz cooking chocolate, melted
4 egg yolks
½ cup granulated sugar
makes about 3¾ cups

1 Make the custard as for Custard Ice Cream, replacing the lemon with the vanilla.

2 Beat the egg yolks with a wire whisk or electric beater. Gradually incorporate the sugar, and continue beating for about 5 minutes until the mixture is pale yellow. Strain the milk. Slowly add it to the egg mixture drop by drop.

3 ▲ Pour the mixture into a double boiler with the melted chocolate. Stir over moderate heat until the water in the pan is boiling, and the custard thickens enough to lightly coat the back of a spoon. Remove from the heat and allow to cool.

4 ▲ Freeze in an ice cream maker, or follow step 5 of Custard Ice Cream, freezing and processing until a smooth consistency has been reached.

INDEX